PRAYERWAYS

*For those who feel
discouraged or distraught,
frightened or frustrated,
angry or anxious,
powerless or purposeless,
overextended or underappreciated,
burned out or just plain
worn out*

PRAYERWAYS

Louis M. Savary
Patricia H. Berne

1817
HARPER & ROW, PUBLISHERS, SAN FRANCISCO
Cambridge, Hagerstown, New York, Philadelphia
London, Mexico City, São Paulo, Singapore, Sydney

FIRST HARPER & ROW EDITION PUBLISHED 1984

Designer: Jim Mennick

Library of Congress Cataloging in Publication Data

Savary, Louis M.
    PRAYERWAYS.
    1. Spiritual life. 2. Conduct of life.
I. Berne, Patricia H., joint author. II. Title.
BV4501.2.S276 1980   248.3'2   80-7737
ISBN 0−06−067068−1
ISBN 0−06−067064−9 (pbk.)

---

84 85 86 87 88 10 9 8 7 6 5 4 3 2 1

Contents

PART IV
Prayerways: Physical Activity

PART V
Prayerways: Interpersonal Presence

Preface

This is a book about staying psychologically and spiritually alive during times of severe personal and social stress. It offers practical suggestions on how to keep caring for yourself and others when everything seems to be going against you and how to keep going, lovingly and prayerfully, during difficult times.

We wrote it for people who are open to the spiritual dimension of life, with or without religious affiliations. Our primary concern in this book is not to discuss religious doctrine or supernatural grace, but to help develop the very natural realms of human spirit and spiritual energy available to all human beings and with which all religions are concerned. We want to help people, especially during times of burnout, dispose their bodies, minds, and spirits for the gifts of God's grace.

We speak of people being "burned out" or being "in burnout" as a shorthand way of describing various conditions of exhaustion, discouragement, and pressure that have become debilitating to a person and have rendered that person incapable of carrying out the everyday affairs of life with an ordinary amount of energy.

During times of severe emotional pressure and burnout, people tend to become confused and sometimes frightened. Familiar styles of praying, working, relating, and loving seem to lose their effectiveness. People feel empty and misplaced; life seems to have lost its value and meaning. Many are tempted to lose respect for themselves and to stop caring for themselves.

At times like these all three human systems—physical, psychological, and spiritual—become vulnerable, and it is necessary to support them as much as possible. Many books have been written to help develop a person's physical and psychological systems. Our intention is to suggest an approach that also deals with the usually missing part, the spiritual system. We present some creative ways of disposing the body, mind, and spirit for fuller life and grace.

We write from our different training and perspectives—one from a psychological orientation, one from a spiritual orientation. Because we feel these two perspectives complement and (at least potentially) coexist in each other, we offer our psychological and spiritual ideas in an integrated "psychospiritual" fashion.

While we tend to focus on the psychospiritual dimensions of working through burnout, our unspoken premise throughout this book is the crucial need for individuals under severe pressure or in burnout to take special care of themselves physically and psychologically. Hence, while we will not again mention a burned-out person's continual need for bodily care, proper nutrition, adequate sleep, cleanliness, sufficient physical exercise, regular periods of rest, vacations, a physician's care, along with the usual psychological and emotional supports of friends, family, and professionals, we do not wish in any way to minimize the importance of these factors in living successfully through times of burnout. In short, for staying fully alive we emphasize the need for burned-out persons to maximize all the normal energy resources available to them.

The term "spiritual energy" is used frequently throughout the book, but many times, as will be evident, we will be talking about both psychological and spiritual energy, or psychospiritual energy.

We believe body, mind, and spirit are all inextricably involved in working with the entire person toward natural wholeness and supernatural holiness. We believe divine grace builds on human nature.

James Michener's novel *The Source* tells the story of a people who built the walls of their city around a wellspring. As long as they utilized this resource within their walls, they could withstand a siege. The people could continue to live centering their lives around their well, which flowed with living water.

We believe people carry within themselves the sources and resources of energy for wholeness, at least potentially. Using these internal energies, calling them forth and strengthening them, is the focus of the prayerful activities we suggest. Actively to build up one's psychospiritual energy system calls for desire, determination, and practice.

Burnout can be a very special time of giftedness. While on the one hand it may be experienced as a dismembering of one's ego, it also offers an opportunity to reassemble one's self as a more functional and loving human being. While it is a time of losing one's life, it can also be a time for finding it again in a new way.

In Christian language, to be in burnout can be an experience likened to being poor in spirit, carrying one's cross, and sharing in Christ's passion. "Come to me all you who are weary, and I will refresh you," said Jesus. Those who are suffering from extreme pressures can invoke God with an urgency possible to no one else. While burnout is a time of woundedness, anguish, and helplessness, it can also be a time of openness to the spirit and to grace. It can be a time of humility and acceptance of one's process toward the wholeness called for by the kingdom. It can be a time, spiritually, for giving up one's desire to be omnipotent and, psychologically, for giving up one's desire to be completely in control of one's life. Above all, burnout can be an opportunity for growth in holiness and wholeness. This book offers ways for you to explore and practice that growth.

This is an attitudinal book as well as a practice book. For example, it develops the attitude that spiritual energy is a very real force in one's life and in the quality of one's life. We believe that each individual is a significant molecule in the larger universe and that one's pain is significant not only for oneself, but for the larger world. From this perspective the activities in the book tend to evoke an internal sense of connectedness with others and with all of nature and ask one to accept one's vulnerability and pain within that larger plan.

We believe people in such pain need to act toward themselves in loving and caring ways; in other words, they need to drink the living water that flows from the divine source within them.

Introduction

Do you sometimes feel discouraged, unappreciated, frustrated, outraged, overwhelmed, worn out, ready to throw in the towel, and unable to face another day? Then this book may help you. Such feelings are often signs not only of a tired body and mind but of a tired spirit.

In these pages we use the term "spiritual" to refer to an essential dimension of every human being. Spiritual energy is a natural energy. It is used at work and play as well as in specifically religious activity. Examples of spiritual energy available to you include creativity, courage, wisdom, empathy, compassion, discernment, inner peace, the ability to affirm yourself, to find meaning in life, and the capacity to carry out your decisions. None of these energies is restricted to the sphere of religious activity. Staying spiritually alive is a problem that faces everyone in all dimensions of life.

People are different. Each person gains and loses energy in different ways. Recently at a workshop participants made a list of things that drained energy from them. As you look at their collective list, consider which items would rank high among your personal energy drains. You may be able to add others of your own. Many physical and psychological drains have the capacity to drain people also of spiritual energies.

Energy Drains

Physical	Psychological	Spiritual
Lack of time	Lack of cooperation	Loss of a sense of self
Lack of money	Lack of humor	Cowardice
Noise	Lack of love	Inability to forgive
Dirty surroundings	Confusion	Feeling unconnected to
Disorder	Misunderstanding	God
Certain people	Hatred	Sense of meaninglessness
Lack of sleep	Anger	Unfulfilled dreams
Poor nutrition	Jealousy	A sense of aimlessness in
Hunger	Envy	life
Mismanagement	Sorrow	Feeling of abandonment
Lack of exercise	Grief	Confusion about personal
Lack of play	Loneliness	commitments
Lack of privacy	Conflicts in	Loss of inner harmony
Illness	relationships	Preoccupation with a
Crowds	Failure in	desire for security
Too many demands	relationships	Continual failure
Unfinished things	Lack of mental	Hypocrisy
Extreme heat or cold	organization	Despair
Extreme dampness	Feeling responsible	Confrontation with
A schedule without rest	Feeling overwhelmed	situations of
periods	Feeling stupid	desperation, poverty,
Shouting	Obsessions	crime, discrimination,
Stereo blaring	Fear and anxiety	cursings and profanity
Long-distance travel	Worry	An uncreative atmosphere
Driving in heavy traffic	Self-punishment	Public apathy
Gloomy weather	Guilt	Personal apathy
Overwhelming number	Expecting failure	Ennui
of little things	Always wanting more	Cruelty
	Preoccupation with	Pessimism
	mistakes	Ingratitude
	Depression	Intractable prejudice
	Poor communication	Indecisiveness
	Feeling let down by	Hopelessness
	others	Lack of intimacy
		Having no alternatives
		Existential aloneness
		Being devalued by others
		Holding grudges
		Worshipping money
		People who don't believe
		in you

The same workshop group then created a corresponding list of experiences that helped put them back in touch with their energy sources. They are listed here in no particular order or categorization. You may be able to add to these lists from your own experience.

Energy Sources

Walking through the woods
Visiting an art museum
Going to the zoo
Working in my garden
Painting a picture
Knitting
Good friends
Silence (peace and quiet)
Dancing
A good book
A vacation
Communion with God
The support of others
Acceptance by others
Getting a hug when I feel alone
A neat office or room
Organized surroundings
Sufficient money
A nature walk
Letting go of my mistakes
Success
Listening to music
A cup of coffee
A cup of tea with a special friend
Hearing someone say they
  love me
Sexual experience
Meditation
Making an important decision
Getting a stroke for a job
Empathizing

Freedom to set my own schedule
Good health
Good nutrition
A good cry
Dinner "out"
Cooperation
Doing something with a friend
Competition
Having a good argument
Doing something courageous
A good night's sleep
Sharing laughter
Being complimented on my
  cooking
Seeing an absorbing movie
Feeling centered
Seeing a meaning in my life
Doing physical exercise
Going to a sports event
Somebody asking my advice
Playing a musical instrument
Driving through the country
Walking on the beach
Sewing
Gardening
Daydreaming
Writing poetry
Achieving an objective
Repairing something
Lending a helping hand
Reading the Bible
Singing

Just as it is valuable to become conscious of your energy drains and how and when they affect you, it is important to get in touch with your energy resources and to use them—as many as you can—especially when times of exhaustion and discouragement are on the horizon.

Throughout this book we suggest ways of transforming these and other energy resources into forms of praying during times of energy drain. Our aim is to offer active prayer to anyone who feels deeply tired, beaten, spent, drained, and used up, but who doesn't want to stay that way, who wants rather to feel alive again—physically, mentally, and spiritually. We suggest that by refreshing ourselves with the energy received in prayer we may become stronger, not only spiritually but also emotionally and physically.

In general this book is for those who feel they need psychospiritual energy but don't know where or how to get it. Its suggestions for reenergizing are presented as prayer forms, though some of them may not feel like traditional ways of praying. We have found that in times of discouragement, frustration, and exhaustion some familiar prayer forms feel unsatisfying and unattractive. At such times of stress fresh prayer activities that involve the whole person—body, mind, and spirit—seem to be more helpful in bringing about openness to and awareness of psychospiritual aliveness.

As experiences in consciousness, these prayerways can help keep you focused on staying psychologically and spiritually alive. If burnout persists no matter what you do, then seek professional help from a physician, counselor, or therapist.

What does it mean to be spiritually alive? What is spiritual energy? How do we obtain it? How do we lose it? How do we get it back? These are some of the questions that lead to the rest of this book.

Part I

Prayerways: Inner Energy and Burnout

Chapter 1

Understanding Burnout

Burnout is a descriptive term people use when they experience progressively severe energy depletion. They feel that, like a charred log in the fireplace, they've run out of energy and are unable to light a fire in themselves. Personal inner resources seem at an end.

Burnout happens everywhere. No way of life is really exempt from it. It is an illness indicative of an imbalance within the totality of an individual. Its symptoms may be experienced physically, psychologically, and spiritually. They may occur on any one or all three of these levels.

Symptoms of Burnout

Physically, burnout may be experienced as fatigue, chronic tiredness, absence of get-up-and-go. Worn out and listless, physically burned-out people seem subject to more than their normal share of colds, viruses, headaches, backaches, nervous tension, and stomachaches. They feel tired, yet they can't sleep; they awaken after a night's sleep, yet they feel unrested; they lack energy to accomplish anything, yet they seem unable to relax. Tasks that seemed easy before now appear as insurmountable obstacles. People who come home from a job they normally enjoy and almost every evening simply collapse for the balance of the night are experiencing burnout. In extreme cases physical burnout may result in physical or nervous exhaustion requiring hospitalization and/or months of recuperation.

Psychologically, burnout may manifest itself in chronic impatience with routine work, carelessness about details, not caring about the outcome of a project, or depression or anxiety as daily feelings. Psychologically burned-out people might characterize themselves as alone, alienated, and bored. They find less and less satisfaction in their work and their personal relationships. They are subject to ungrounded fears and often remark, "What's the use." Most days have an oppressive sameness about them. They worry excessively, are easily distracted, and have difficulty concentrating. Encounters that always seemed easy before now seem fraught with complexities and fear of failure and rejection. When an administrator finds herself sitting at her desk unable to face the day's mail and afraid to pick up a ringing telephone for fear it will bear another problem, she is experiencing burnout. In extreme situations psychological burnout may result in suicidal feelings and/or a nervous breakdown.

Spiritually burned-out people symptomatically cannot seem to summon up hope in their life and work; they have chronic fits of doubt about their own worth and effectiveness; they begin to feel unsure about the honesty or goodness of their decisions; they lack courage to take even ordinary risks; they lose all sense of freshness and creativity in their work and relationships; they find it almost impossible to forgive themselves and others in order to move forward; they feel the meaning and purpose of their life eroding; they gradually lose a sense of self and an ability to affirm themselves; they can no longer act assertively (or, if they do, their words and actions are usually infected with defensiveness, paternalism, arrogance, or excessive authoritarianism); they begin losing the inner strength to make and realize personal commitments. Signs of a zest for life, such as curiosity, wonder, sensuality, sensory awareness, sexuality, affectivity, joy, playfulness, humor, and love of nature and animals tend to dry up. Burned-out cases almost forget what it feels like to be enthusiastically alive; they feel an increasing need to escape decision making and to avoid conflict or even confrontation; they become less and less certain of anything—principles, convictions, procedures, and values. They often become very narrowly focused and self-absorbed; they experience loneliness despite regular contact with many persons; they find relationships that involve intimacy and personal growth difficult and tend to avoid self-revelatory encounters. They lose almost all awareness of awe and mystery, of God's presence, of the unity of all things.

Burnout as a Process

Although burnout symptoms may first be noticed on any level—physical, psychological, or spiritual—burnout is a dysfunction whose symptoms normally occur progressively in stages: first, physically (for example, in chronic tiredness or bodily complaints); then, psychologically (for example, in being bored, not caring about important people or projects, or going around feeling depressed for no apparent reason); and finally, spiritually (for example, in losing hope, losing a sense of self, feeling helplessly indecisive). In its process, burnout is an illness that eventually affects body, mind, and spirit.

"To say that someone is in burnout," writes psychologist Michael D. Mitchell, "is to say that he or she is somewhere in a progressive process of fatigue and depletion of personal resources." *

Finding Burnout

While the personal symptoms just described are important as detectors of burnout, the roots of the problem usually lie else-

* "Consultant Burnout," *The 1977 Annual Handbook for Group Facilitators*, ed. J. E. Jones and J. W. Pfeiffer (LaJolla, Cal.: University Associates, 1977), p. 143.

where. It is difficult to name causes for burnout, but we can point to occasions or situations that tend to foster it. The following are four of the commonest situations that seem to give rise to burnout.

Difficult transitions are the first and most obvious occasions. While most people think the world will never change and hope they will not have to change, everyone acknowledges that change itself is life's one predictable constant. Because of jobs, people are uprooted and must set up new homes in unfamiliar, sometimes unfriendly, places. Because of sickness and death, family members must often radically alter their lifestyles. Many people, following heart attack or major surgery, have to make the transition to a new self-image and certain physical restrictions. Others learn they will have to adjust their lives to the effects of cancer, brain tumors, permanent injuries, and incurable diseases. When individuals, neighborhoods, and even nations change their attitudes and values, the transition can be difficult and threatening for many. Things that formerly were predictable—teachers never went out on strike, nurses always wore uniforms, sons and daughters didn't publicly cohabite with partners of the opposite sex—are no longer predictable. Even the unchanging churches have changed. Moral and civil laws that once seemed clear and ironclad are challenged, reinterpreted, or disregarded. Everyone goes on strike now. Women assert their rights. Decisions like getting married, which used to be lifetime ones, are now often temporary and provisional. Divorce, death, marriage, job changes, separations, moves, loss of friendship, and acknowledging that one will have to live with severe illness in oneself or a loved one are all stressful transitions that can trigger burnout. They don't always trigger it, but often enough they do.

Second, *high stress situations* that have no release valve may occur on jobs or in relationships that produce continual frustration or failure: the frustrated parent who must ask a child to do something many times and it still doesn't get done; the intensive care nurse who continually watches people die despite her vigilant care; a spouse who is a chronic complainer and constantly critical of a partner. Other high stress situations include continual financial drains and the threat of financial collapse, a long-term illness in the family, alcoholism, drug addiction, imprisonment, hunger, pain, noise, and traffic. Administrators generally live with high stress trying to keep an organization running and adequately staffed. Many people find they will have to live the rest of their lives with chronic physical and psychological pain.

Also qualifying as high stress with no escape are situations where people consistently feel overwhelmed or devoured. Their life is full of demands from others. They seem to be living at least three lives; everyone wants a piece of them; they can't say no yet they have no time to do what they have already said yes to; they can't seem to do their job; there is no way to earn enough money to pay existing bills. They feel a sense of helplessness in the face of events—large or small. A ten-minute favor seems overpoweringly difficult to manage. They dread hearing their telephone ring. They are riding a merry-go-round, helplessly fastened to an up-and-down horse, and there is no getting off.

Third, *high ambiguity situations* can also give rise to burnout. While transitions take people, forcibly or willingly, from one place to another and high stress situations keep people stuck in one place or in an endless cycle, high ambiguity situations are those that never seem to resolve themselves. In fact, there seems to be no resolution available. People in this place cannot seem to find the necessary clarity and information on which to base decisions. Errors, sometimes costly ones, seem inevitable. People here feel pulled toward and pushed away from something at the same time; they feel frozen and fearful, unable to respond. They may end up doing something just for the sake of doing something. They cannot direct their own lives since ambiguity and confusion sit at either side of their every choice.

Those who cannot cope well with ambiguity will tend consistently to avoid responsibility; they are happy and relieved to see somebody else do it. Ambiguous relationships—at home, on the job, or among friends—tend to inject in some a dread of participating in events, parties, or meetings that only a short time ago they eagerly anticipated. Now they can't wait for them to be over.

Fourth, *nonreciprocity*, according to Mitchell, is the root of all burnout. Nonreciprocity involves an unequal balance in relationship. In some relationships the one subject to burnout is the one who consistently gives, helps, supports, listens, and empathizes. This one makes a great investment in the relationship and gets little gratitude, feedback, or even acknowledgment from the other. Nonreciprocal relationships occur commonly between parent and children, teacher and students, social worker and clients, salespeople and customers, clergy and parishioners, law enforcement officers and citizens, therapists and patients, and political officeholders and voters. A fatiguing sense of inequality among peers may also exist, for example, between spouses, siblings, relatives, coworkers, or students. Nonreciprocity also occurs where there is prejudice or discrimination because of race, creed, class, family, nationality, sex, education, credentials, and other factors. "Although nonreciprocity is inevitable and acceptable," writes Mitchell, "it is also draining. No one can function long in a helping profession without feeling its impact."*

Living Through Difficult Situations

When more than one occasion for burnout is felt at the same time, the chances of burnout are probably greater. It is not difficult to find people who are living with more than one, or even all four situations. For example, a mother caring for her children who never say "thanks" experiences *nonreciprocity;* because her husband adamantly refuses to talk about their continually deteriorating relationship, she experiences *high stress;* with her mother who just had a stroke, can no longer live alone

* Ibid.

in her own apartment, and is coming to live with them, she experiences a *difficult transition;* and at work her boss continues to make sexual advances at her, which puts her in a *high ambiguity* situation.

Some people are able to live through extremely difficult situations without burning out. How do they do it? Prevention is, of course, the best way: an ongoing program of staying alive and well—in body, mind, and spirit.

For those who are already in burnout, it helps to remember that any illness is something to respond to in a holistic way. This means that an illness is to be viewed as part of an individual's growth process. It is not only a signal of imbalance that needs to be treated but a call to concern for one's health and wholeness, pointing the way to possible and needed transformations in one's way of being.

It is important to remember that even chronic symptoms are not sufficient to assert that this or that must simply be a case of burnout. Therefore whenever there is any doubt and the symptoms seem unusually prolonged, professional care is strongly recommended.

Chapter 2

Understanding Spiritual Energy

Identifying Spiritual Energy

What is spiritual energy? How does it differ from physical energy or mental energy? Is it different from what religious people call "grace"? These are a few of the questions asked about spiritual energy. The answers aren't as clear as we might like. But we do know that people can think about spiritual energy and experience its effects just as naturally as they can experience physical and psychological energies.

Energy basically means *the ability to do something.* Thus electrical energy means the ability to do electrical work; chemical energy means the ability to produce chemical reactions; physical energy means the ability to generate measurable effects; psychological energy means the ability to do mental work and exert emotional effort; and spiritual energy refers to an ability to exercise and activate various capacities of the human spirit.

The ebb and flow of physical energies are probably the clearest to identify. For example, when people awaken after a needed sleep, they feel rested; perhaps a headache has gone away, too, or some muscle soreness. When people step out of the shower and feel full of energy or when they feel strength returning as they eat, these clearly focus the physical side of human energy.

Mentally, the ability to solve a complex mathematical problem, to recall historical names, dates, and places, or to analyze the results of a medical examination are signs of mental energy at work. So are expressions of love, anger, guilt, grief, delight, fear, and humor—all of these are raw material for the therapist, whose domain is psychological energy.

Finally, there are capacities of the human spirit that go beyond both the physical and psychological. For example, forgiveness, courage, compassion, willpower, hope, wisdom, inner joy, and peace are human capacities the psychologist recognizes but cannot explain simply in terms of psychological variables. So we attribute these activities principally to the human spirit.

The burnout victim may experience incapacities in any or all of the three human dimensions. Those related to the spiritual seem to be least known and most often forgotten in treating burnout. Only when people learn to identify and specify their spiritual activities can they begin to recognize where their spiritual energies are stronger or weaker.

Spiritual Energies, Virtues, and Grace

There seem to be many different kinds of spiritual energy. The Eastern traditions appear to be more sophisticated in their awareness of spiritual energy and its workings than those in the West. At least it seems that the Eastern traditions treat the energizing capacities of the human spirit more explicitly than we do in the West. In Western traditions spiritual energies are usually discussed as virtues. However, the sense of the Latin word *virtus* as a potential, power, or energy has receded in favor of virtue as a quality of behaving and responding. Thus the virtue of modesty, instead of being viewed as an inner source of energy, is seen as a style of behavior or dress.

In Christian tradition many spiritual energies (or virtues) are presented as "gifts" or graces. Thus there are the many gifts of the Holy Spirit, discussed in Paul's First Letter to the Corinthi-

ans, Chapters 12–13, or the nine "fruits" of the Holy Spirit—
love, joy, peace, patience, kindness, goodness, faithfulness,
gentleness, and self-control—which Paul presented in Gala-
tians 5:22–23.

When one views spiritual gifts as fonts of energy—much as
we view the sun, wind, tides, waterfalls, petroleum, coal, or
wood as sources of energy—it is clear they need to be recognized, used, adapted, processed, worked at, cooperated with,
and developed in order to be fully effective.

Often in burnout it is not that the supply of spiritual fuel has
run out; rather, it appears that we block ourselves from our
sources of spiritual energy, we are unaware of their presence,
or we try to force them into uses for which they were never in-
tended and where they prove ineffective.

It may be helpful to those dealing with burnout to look at
some of the key kinds of spiritual energies people need and
use. The energies described here are those related to seven classical spiritual energy centers, called *chakras* in certain Eastern
traditions.

Transmitting Life Transmitting life is the basic spiritual
energy available to humans. It is often symbolized by the color
red, as in blood or wine. Some expressions of transmitting life
include the ability to expend effort, often in great surges; to
work creatively with matter; to work patiently despite resistance; to procreate; to express sexuality; to enjoy sensuality; to
use hands, feet, and body in expressing life, as in dancing,
painting, or playing a musical instrument; to find joy and peace
in life; and to be in touch with the life force, the *elan vital*.

At this energy center, the opening for which is said to be located near the base of the spine, physical and spiritual energies
join forces to transform and transmit life. People open at this
center seem to possess boundless energy. In them the energy to
transmit life is expressed sometimes quietly and peacefully,
sometimes exuberantly and freeflowing. In contrast, in many
burnouts this energy seems to move frenetically and as if it
were forced and compulsively driven.

When burnout involves physical exhaustion or an inability to do your work in your usual relaxed and creative ways, it may be related to this basic spiritual energy.

To keep aware of your need for energies related to transmitting life, it may help to focus your attention on the color red. Think red during your day. Wear red clothing; add some red decoration to your room; notice people who wear red; and choose red foods and drinks. Whenever you connect with something red, consciously in a prayer invite the life energy you need to enter you and flow through you. Let the color red, wherever you see it, signal you to open yourself to the life energies that can keep you alive.

Self-Affirmation and Self-Awareness The center for the spiritual energies of self-affirmation and self-awareness, associated physically with the lower intestines,* is often symbolized by the color orange. Some expressions of self-affirmation energy include the ability to see oneself as worthwhile, valuable, and unique; to have a positive self-image; to say "I am" or "I exist"; and to affirm the integration of one's body, mind, and spirit.

Burnout victims are often tempted to devalue themselves, to experience a sense of ego loss or identity loss. To break out of burnout it seems necessary to possess self-value or some sense of identity. This energy center enables you to affirm that you are human, that though you are finite and fallible, you are still competent and likable, that you are called to friendship, that you are called to love, that you are a child of God, and that you can say to others, "I'm OK—You're OK."

In times of burnout you may be tempted to settle for equating your identity with some role you play or a social mask you wear; to settle for being a good girl or a nice guy; to be what other people want you to be; to claim that you are powerless; to

---

* The place in the human body where this energy is believed to enter, in the area of the bowels or lower intestines at about hip level, is called *hara* by the Japanese. For them this is where the self, or center of one's being, resides. Thus *hara-kiri*, a form of suicide by disembowelment formerly practiced by Japanese nobility, symbolized the cutting out of one's self or center.

deny, distort, or depreciate who you are; to believe no longer in yourself, in your competence, in your compassion.

Burnout people lacking this self-affirmation energy are at times tempted to let go of human relationships, feeling unworthy of them, and to avoid approaching God. If your burnout involves the inability to affirm yourself, you may want to focus on the color orange, which symbolizes this energy: orange fruits, orange flowers, orange-covered books, orange-colored automobiles. Use orange towels. Carry with you some little orange-colored thing you can touch and look at from time to time. Each time the color orange makes you aware that you need the energy of self-affirmation, let yourself say a short prayer that you be open to receive this energy. Let yourself feel a longing for awareness of your value and uniqueness.

Courage Courage, symbolized by yellow—the color both of cowardice and courage—is a crucial energy needed by burned-out people. As psychiatrist Rollo May defines it, courage is not the opposite of discouragement or despair; it is the ability to go forward *despite* discouragement or despair. It is closely related to hope.

Expressions of courage include the ability to forgive oneself, as well as others; to take risks in creativity and in relationships; to move forward even in times of failure; to face seemingly overwhelming fears; to accept one's own limits and inadequacies, as well as those of others; and to enter new stages of personal growth and inner exploration.

For Jesus the courage to forgive and to ask forgiveness opened people to a change of heart. Not least among forgiveness's effects is the ability to form liberating relationships with one's enemies, including the enemies who dwell within one's own psyche. Forgiveness, or at least the readiness to forgive, is a special spiritual quality. God is merciful and forgiving to all, Jesus says, "he is kind to the ungrateful and the selfish" (Luke 6:35). And in another place the spiritual energy of forgiveness is attributed to God, who "makes the sun rise on those who are evil and on those who are good and sends rain on the just and the unjust" (Matt. 5:45–46).

The opposite of courage is cowardice. The coward is paralyzed by fear, and cannot move forward. Burnout victims commonly experience themselves as failures, discouraged, despairing, losers, or useless. Hence their need for courage is paramount: courage, first to forgive themselves, next to forgive those who may have occasioned the burnout, then to move forward.

Anne Sullivan, Helen Keller's teacher, struggled for months without success to teach her blind and deaf young charge even a single word. Yet each day Anne would start afresh, courageously. And one day Helen did learn her first word, "water." After that breakthrough Helen learned words as fast as Anne could teach her. Anne's courage paid off.

Physically, the center for courage energy is located in the solar plexus. Thus people speak of a courageous person as one who has "guts" and of a coward as one who lacks "guts." People who tend to lose courage energy sometimes manifest their condition by physical symptoms, including stomachaches, ulcers, or other internal disorders.

Those lacking courage can let everything yellow, symbolic color of courage, remind them that this spiritual energy is available to them. They can imagine themselves inhaling the color yellow from the atmosphere, thereby opening themselves to receive this special energy.

Compassion Compassion, or caring love, is the spiritual energy that gives people the ability to be *inter*personal, to *react* emotionally, to be thoughtful, to reach out in friendship, to empathize, to be generous, and to experience oneness with people, animals, and nature. It is energy associated with the heart. When burnout is focused here, it may be experienced as blocked emotions, hatred that expresses a wish to be cut off or separated from another, misunderstandings that are jealously guarded, heartbreak and overwhelming sadness, hardheartedness and lack of sensitivity, inability to care, mistrust in general, and an avoidance of friends.

When flowing, this energy enables people to let go of hatred, mistrust, and misunderstanding, to express their feelings of kindness, to reestablish bonds of friendship, and to be open and generous. This energy also enables persons to integrate their whole body and lovingly to govern their bodies.

This spiritual energy was clearly primary and superior to all others for Jesus. Love—compassionate love—is his single commandment, the wellspring of his life, the foundation of the life of his community, and the ultimate key to the kingdom of God. Jesus would measure a person's moral goodness by what "comes out of his heart" (see Matt. 15:18). He found mere juridical obedience morally unsatisfactory and wanted rather a commitment of the heart. For Jesus the heart is the spokesman or governor of the person.

In the Old Testament, Yahweh makes the human heart the receptacle of his love and his promises. Through the mouth of Jeremiah the prophet, the Lord says, "This is the covenant I will make with the house of Israel after those days: I will put my law within them, and I will write it upon their hearts; and I will be their God and they shall be my people" (Jer. 31:31).

In New Testament times not only Jesus but also his believing community stress the centrality of the heart. Paul the Apostle clearly states that the Father relates primarily to the heart. God's love, Paul explains, is "poured into human hearts through the Holy Spirit" (Rom. 5:5). And in another place he describes the effects of faith as "having the eyes of your heart enlightened" (Eph. 1:18). In the Old and New Testaments the heart is mentioned over a thousand times.

One traditional Christian prayer form is called the prayer of the heart. In this form the words of a prayer are first understood by the mind, then the understanding mind is placed in the heart (the seat of the emotions) and the prayer is spoken by the heart. Thus in the prayer of the heart, the mind and heart are brought together in the heart, and it is the heart that prays. Perhaps the best-known prayer of the heart is the Jesus Prayer; of its many versions the commonest is "Lord Jesus Christ, Son of God, have mercy on me, a sinner." It is voiced from the heart, uttered over and over hundreds, even thousands of times. A very simple prayer to open the heart center involves breathing from the heart. Use your imagination to picture the area around your heart opening itself to breathe in and out. While breathing in this way, invite the spiritual energy of compassion to enter.

For those who wish to open their heart, the symbolic color of compassion and openness is green, the color nature spreads most profusely over the earth.

Choice Power and Decisiveness The spiritual center for the energies of choice power and decisiveness, symbolized by sky blue color and physically located in the throat area, is principally the domain of energies associated with the Holy Spirit and the will. According to Jesus, it is the spirit's task to make God's kingdom a reality on earth, which means to carry out God's will for humanity.

When people are open to this kind of spiritual energy, they discover in themselves power: to choose effectively, and wisely, to carry out their decisions, to make personal commitments, to grasp the meaning of the kingdom, to discern how the kingdom is being realized in oneself and in others, and to speak with wisdom. It may also be described as the energy that makes the kingdom *manifest*. In the Lord's Prayer this spiritual energy is revealed in the petition "Thy kingdom come, thy will be done on earth as it is in heaven." Because of its relation to the kingdom, this energy center provides capacities for developing morality and ethics. Because this center is located in the throat, the part that connects a person's heaven (mind) and earth (body), it provides the energy to integrate the whole person— mind and body—enabling the person to act as a totality, not with body and mind split.

This spiritual energy center also releases spiritual and mental creativity to complement the physical and material creativity associated with the energy of transmitting life. Some other rather unusual gifts connected with this spiritual energy center include prophecy, speaking in tongues, interpretation of tongues, and other capacities usually associated with the baptism of the Holy Spirit.

Burnout victims may experience a blocking of the spiritual

energies related to choice power and decisiveness when they find they habitually resist or avoid making decisions, when they frequently cannot choose between alternatives, when they cannot see even in ordinary circumstances what would or would not promote God's kingdom, when they consistently cannot carry out even simple decisions, or when they repeatedly cannot exercise even their ordinary authority.

To become aware of this spiritual energy and to open yourself to it, surround yourself with sky blue color. Wear it, decorate things with it, and notice it in advertisments, painting, and nature. Each time you consciously attend to the color sky blue, open yourself to the energy of the Holy Spirit. Another simple way to connect with the sources of this energy is to repeat in mantra fashion the petition of the Lord's Prayer: "Thy kingdom come, thy will be done on earth as it is in heaven."

Spiritual Awareness and Meaning The energies of spiritual awareness and meaning, associated with the color deep blue or indigo in the rainbow, are focused in the area around the eyes. In spiritual literature these energies are often described in terms of wisdom and discernment. Their function is to help people comprehend or grasp reality from a perspective of universal awareness. Thus these energies are often referred to as the special domain of God's word or God's son, the *Logos*, the Greek word for word, truth, meaning, and understanding. They also support and deepen the energies of the mental faculties: the ability to understand, to discriminate, to find or give meaning, to grasp truth, to give names to things, to be aware, to evaluate and decide, to use words in explaining knowledge, and to grow in depth of one's individual consciousness. Here in this spiritual center is where we hear the voice of our teacher, master, or guru; it is the center of our spiritual eyes and a meeting place with the divine.

Those whose burnout affects their spiritual awareness energies will probably find it difficult to find meaning and purpose in their life, to discriminate truth from falseness, to stay conscious and aware of what is happening in themselves and around them, accurately to evaluate facts and situations, and to understand or explain what is happening. Burnout here may manifest itself by a wish to retreat to unconsciousness, sleep, or daydream, especially about the past and what might have been, a wish to avoid reality and a reluctance to admit what is happening, a wish not to hear the word of God or the voice of one's inner guide.

To open oneself to *Logos* one may picture one's head surrounded by an aura of deep blue. One may ask God to open one's spiritual eyes. These are the kind of eyes Jesus referred to when he said, "Let those who have eyes to see, open them," (cf. Mark 4:9).

Transcendent Consciousness This seventh (for some, the highest) form of spiritual energy, transcendent consciousness, is traditionally believed to enter us through the crown of the head. Symbolized by the royal color, purple, it expresses a capacity for transcendent experience; for fullest growth and maturity; for consciousness of being, life, and existence in their fullest meaning; for the expansion of consciousness; for broadening perspectives and for overcoming prejudice; for enabling people to see through conflicts to their resolution; for helping people deal with paradox and live within apparent contradiction; for awareness of consummate being where the union of opposites is reached; for transcending time and death; for controlling the other six centers of spiritual energy; for being in touch with the "heaven" of one's own consciousness—that place of totality, completeness, unity, integration, and fullness that waits to be discovered and evolved within us; for realizing the kingdom of God within oneself; for realizing that one's body is a temple of the living God; and for realizing one is a son or daughter of God and possesses divine life. It is the spiritual energy normally associated with God the Father and offers those who possess it the ability to view events from an eternal perspective.

When a person's seventh energy center is fully opened, the purple color is believed to change to gold. Thus saints and holy people in the Western tradition are depicted with a golden halo or aura surrounding the top of their head. In the Eastern traditions openness to the fullness of consciousness is sometimes symbolized by a protuberance or bulge on the top of the head, most often seen on statues of Buddhas or of those who have reached fullest enlightenment.

Burnout victims affected by problems with this seventh kind of energy usually experience it as a lack of perspective. They may lose their sense of connection with God and God's kingdom. They may feel prayer and meditation are meaningless and find themselves preferring instead to get lost in the busyness of everyday affairs. They may find themselves experiencing a narrowness of vision, defensively closing themselves off from freedom and creative exploration in realms of consciousness, in realms of ethics and moral behavior, and in realms of relationships. Instead, for the burnout victim old prejudices regarding groups of people or individuals begin to dominate conversation and actions. Out of the ordinary responses in others that might have been understandable and acceptable just a short time ago now appear improper, intolerable, or threatening.

Seemingly paradoxical behaviors in others that used to be easy to integrate now seem clearly contradictory. Instead of unifying things that seem to be opposites, the burnout victim may tend to emphasize their contrast or demand corresponding either/or behavior: you may do either this or that, but not both.

Lack of transcendent awareness is saddest of all for the burned-out person who is commonly a very devout or religious person accustomed to frequent meditation and prayer and their accompanying satisfying feelings. They experience a kind of depressive emptiness, as if God had withdrawn. The divine presence can no longer be felt, no matter how hard one tries to "do everything right." Meditative techniques that always used to "work" seem now totally ineffective. Familiar prayers that used to guarantee a sense of God's presence seem empty and worthless.

Burnout and Dark Night

An important distinction here needs to be made between burnout, which is a physical-psychological-spiritual condition brought about by inappropriately exhaustive use of one's energies, and the "dark night of the soul," described by the mystics, which is a natural part of the growth process in spiritual development and usually happens even when a person is well energized physically, emotionally, and spiritually. The dark night arrives unpredictably, without being caused or brought on by the person, while the onset of burnout is predictable and usually brought on by persons themselves. The dark night is a spiritually healthy, though often painful, process; burnout is primarily unhealthy and therefore undesirable. The dark night cannot be prevented by those who are ready for it, since it is a natural stage in spiritual development; in contrast burnout, which is an illness, can be prevented. Although many burnout victims learn important lessons through their suffering, burnout is not a recommended technique for higher learning.

Summary

It may be helpful to summarize here schematically the seven classical energy centers with their corresponding energies and rainbow colors. When an energy center is fully opened, certain spiritual masters explain, the color primarily associated with its energy is transformed. Beside each basic color in the diagram is listed the color the energy seems to have when the center is fully open. A correspondence between the seven spiritual energies and the seven petitions of the Lord's Prayer is also suggested.*

* For a more complete treatment of this correspondence see Samuel P. Reinke, "Using the Lord's Prayer in Meditation," *Spiritual Frontiers,* 3:4 (Autumn 1971), pp. 202–214, and Louis M. Savary, S.J., "The Lord's Prayer Centering Meditation," a cassette produced by NCR Cassettes, P.O. Box 281, Kansas City, Mo. 64141.

Summary of Spiritual Energies, Their Centers, Their Colors, and Their Correspondence in the Lord's Prayer

Spiritual Energies	Location of Spiritual Centers	Primary Color	Color When Opened	Correspondence in Lord's Prayer
Transcendent consciousness	7 Crown of head	Purple	Gold	Our Father who art in heaven
Spiritual awareness and meaning	6 Brow	Indigo	Purple	Hallowed be thy name
Choice power and decisiveness	5 Throat	Sky blue	Gray	Thy Kingdom come, Thy will be done, *etc.*
Compassionate love	4 Heart	Green	Pale (color of rain clouds)	Deliver us from evil
Courage	3 Solar plexus	Yellow	Red	forgive us our trespasses, *etc.*
Self-affirmation and self-awareness	2 Lower intestines	Orange	Black	Lead us not into temptation
Transmitting life	1 Base of spine	(Blood) Red	White	Give us this day our daily bread (and wine)

Chapter 3

Relaxing and Centering

The secret of relaxing is that the body, mind, and spirit all know how to relax by themselves and they do it almost automatically if given the chance. Physical and mental relaxation is at the root of spiritual growth. It is difficult to relax the heart if the body is tense or the mind is anxious. In this sense relaxing seems to be an indispensable prerequisite for disposing yourself for meditation and contemplation or, for that matter, for any holistic human activity you do.

Let your relaxing prayerfully begin by offering your body to God. To do this you might simply say, "Here's my body, God. Let your spirit live in it and fill it with the energy to serve you today."

To begin relaxing, posture and breath are the first and most important items to be cared for. Any posture is acceptable for relaxing provided your spine is kept straight, which can be done while sitting, standing, kneeling, or lying on your back (with knees bent). The erect spine allows blood to flow and breath to move most freely.

Breathing properly involves use of the diaphragm, not merely the chest muscles. When you're lying on your back, proper breathing will cause your stomach to rise and fall. Place a hand

gently on your stomach so you can clearly tell if you are
breathing properly. As long as your hand rises and falls, no
matter how little, your breathing is acceptable for inducing relaxation.

The simplest form of inducing relaxation is to focus on your
breathing. Simply observe your breathing process, without
analyzing, judging, or evaluating it. Observing is enough of a
psychological activity to occupy the mind. To bring in the
spiritual dimension, acknowledge each breath as a gift from
God and offer each breath back to God in gratitude for the gift
of life. Breath is a sign of life and a symbol of the spirit. To observe your breathing is a symbolic way of watching your spirit
at work within you.

Another form of prayerfully relaxing is to watch with gratitude the cleansing and nourishing effects of breath in your
body. As you inhale, let yourself be filled with breath and spirit; as you exhale, let yourself release whatever is holding you in
tension or under pressure. With your imagination picture your
body releasing its stress and slowly relaxing. Don't try to force
any change in your breathing pattern. Do nothing but watch it
and use your imagination. You might picture the Holy Spirit
filling you with loving energy or visualize it like a transparent
light filling you up inside. If you are especially tense or depressed, you may wish to repeat a relaxation process three or
four times during your day.

It is helpful to be conscious of a variety of activities that
might tend to relax you. For example, among the things you
may find relaxing are taking a bath, jogging, shampooing your
hair, giving yourself a foot massage, taking a nap, walking
around the block, jumping rope, listening to music, going to a
shopping center, looking at something beautiful, sipping a cup
of tea, trying on clothing, or dancing. Just about any activity
can be a way into relaxing prayer for somebody or other. As
long as an activity qualifies as something that can help relax
you, you may use it prayerfully.

Mental and Physical Tension

Different people use different things to relax them at different times. For example, people whose bodies are quiet but whose minds are tense may find that watching television, going to a film, or playing chess helps relax them. In contrast, people whose minds are quiet but whose bodies are tense may find that walking, jogging, yoga, or dancing is their best relaxant.

The rule is that if your tension is expressing itself physically, you may need to do something physical in order to relax; if your tension is expressing itself mentally, you may need to do something else mental to relax.

While those whose minds and bodies are only minimally tense may be able to get involved in simple meditation experiences, those whose minds and bodies are under severe pressure may, in order to begin relaxing, need to focus body and mind totally, for example, in playing tennis or doing some activity that requires both physical and mental concentration.

The words "heal," "whole," and "holy" all come from the same root English word. Relaxing is the first step on the road to healing, wholeness, and holiness.

Relaxing is also the first step in meditation in general. The more relaxed you are in body and mind, the more open you are to hearing the inner movements of the spirit.

Feeling Lost

One of the commonest experiences during the onset of burnout and during burnout itself is the sense of being "lost." Psychologically, this "lost" feeling is experienced when you lose a sense of your ego or identity. You can almost honestly say you don't know who you are. This experience is very different from amnesia, which is a total blocking of memory. When you're psychologically lost, you don't forget your name or facts about your life, as you usually do in amnesia; it's that the facts and the names seem to have no reality and vitality to them. Like ghosts, they are present but they can't be touched or felt. You carry on the routine of living, but you feel little sense of identity; there is little to affirm about your self. It is hard to answer the question, "Who am I?"

This "lost" feeling may also infect your spiritual identity, as when your heart or soul seems to be in a tunnel or in some place of darkness. You seem to have lost your sense of direction in life. The things you do seem meaningless, purposeless. One who is spiritually lost finds it hard to answer the questions, "Why am I?" or "What am I for?"

People who in childhood did not experience much self-esteem and the esteem of others seem prone to getting lost, psychologically and spiritually. The lost feeling is often an anxious and frightful place to be in.

When someone is lost, they want to be found. They want to find their way home—physically, psychologically, and spiritually. Being at home in a spiritual sense is what is meant by being "centered." The process of getting centered is called centering. To be spiritually lost means to be disconnected from your center. To become centered means to find your self at home again.

To Be Centered

In its fullest meaning to be centered means not only to be at home, to be totally present to myself, but also to be in touch with my energies and the way they are flowing at the present moment. Ram Dass, in his book title, *Be Here Now*, captured the essence of being centered. Centering involves *being* rather than doing; it is a very unbusy process. Centering has to do with being in touch with energy sources, not necessarily using them. Centering involves being *here*, inside yourself, at home, fully present, not wandering off somewhere in your imagination. Centering also focuses on *now*, this very moment, not on memories of the past or expectations of the future. So, really to *be here now* is to be centered.

Learning to center, like learning any skill, is usually a bit difficult at first and may take many minutes. But as you practice, each act of centering becomes easier, and eventually you will be able to center yourself in a few moments. Discover those ways of centering that work best for you and use them. Centering is a spiritually beneficial practice whether or not you're burned out.

A very effective way to get centered, also useful when you are near burnout, is to focus on a single thing: a flower, a leaf, a rock, a bracelet, a ring, a shoe, a matchstick, a drop of water, a cup, or whatever. It is easier to get centered—to BE HERE NOW—if your object is something simple and tangible.

Another way of naturally centering is to grow aware of your body. If centering means coming home, and home is where your body is, then you can get centered by becoming aware of your self in your body. Start, for example, by becoming conscious of what your body is *touching*, and thank God for that awareness. For example, you might begin, "I can feel my feet against the floor. Thanks for my feet and the floor, Lord." You may explore other touching parts of yourself, the different temperatures on different parts of your skin, the gentle air current that touches the hair on your face. As you do this exercise, you will begin to grow quiet and to feel in touch with your body and the atmosphere around you. Such a state of mind may not qualify as a very deep centering, but for someone in burnout this physical centering itself is an accomplishment.

One easy breathing technique for centering that is practiced in yoga involves watching your breath. Step one is to select a specific part of your body involved in the breathing process, say, your left nostril. Step two is simply to watch the air (using your imagination-attention) as it goes in and out passing through your nostrils. It's that simple. Do this for five minutes and you will be much more centered than when you began.

You may then offer your centering self to God, being grateful to God that you are reaching a state of physical and emotional relaxation where you are once more in touch with yourself and "at home."

Still another way of restfully centering is to go to a favorite outdoor place. Most people can find such a special, quiet place relatively near work or home: a mountain, a park, a brook, or a wooded path. To get centered, go to the place when you have a free period of time. (Some will need half an hour at least; others will be able to center themselves in a few minutes.) Then simply stand or sit there, letting yourself grow quiet inside. Allow the good feelings you associate with this place to fill you. Breathe its atmosphere; look around reflectively; listen to its harmonies; and let yourself fit into the scene.

One woman, like the mature Siddhartha in Hesse's novel, said her favorite centering place was near flowing water. "When I get really stressed," she said, "I sit by the creek, which has been a favorite place of mine on our farm since childhood. I simply watch the creek. Sometimes I talk to it and listen to what it says to me. I think God put that creek there for me."

If you can't get to your favorite outdoor place easily, find a restful place—it may be your room, the basement, the back porch, or the attic in your home. Then use your imagination to transport you in spirit to your favorite outdoor place.

It's best if you do your imagining at a time and in a place where you will not be disturbed. One man found he could enjoy these unbothered moments in his workshop; another found asylum in his car; a woman found an empty neighborhood church whose door remained unlocked during the day.

Centering for Children

In teaching centering to children, it helps to capture their imagination. Likewise for adults. A meditation teacher, Yolanda Casteneda, says that in helping children to get centered she asks them to imagine themselves as coffeepots perking.

"Picture a coffeepot stem coming up through your body and out the top of your head," she tells the children. "See your energies perking up from inside you and bubbling out the top." If the perking coffeepot image helps you get centered, then by all means use it. With children having energy is very important. For them to be centered means to be especially in touch with the flow of energies present in them.

Frequent Centering

The effectiveness of centering is enhanced if you do it consistently and frequently. Normally, even during nonstressful periods, centering is recommended twice each day. In time of burnout more frequent practice of centering is helpful, even if only short periods are available for it. Remember, if you're near burnout, exhausted and discouraged, it's your job to *stay alive.* Nobody else will do it for you. Your car, your typewriter, your furniture, and your house are all replaceable—you aren't. Staying fully alive is your most important task.

Centering with Mantras

"When I'm in lots of distress," said a woman, "I tend to hold my head in my hands, rock back and forth in my chair, and repeat over and over my single-word prayer to God, 'Please, please, please.'"

"When I'm in pain or very worried," said an older woman, "I like to say the Lord's Prayer over and over. It seems to comfort me."

A lawyer's favorite prayer in time of stress is the Jesus Prayer, "Lord Jesus Christ, Son of God, have mercy on me, a sinner," which he repeats under his breath many times a day.

All three of these people are using a kind of centering process called a *mantra.* A mantra is simply a set of words or sounds that seems to produce some effect in us when repeated over and over, either silently or aloud. An energy releaser, a mantra may be used effectively in times of stress, grief, loss, fear, tension, and pain (physical, psychological, or spiritual).

A mantra may be employed anywhere at any time, since it can be performed silently or aloud. It is primarily an activity of the heart. "I used my favorite mantra—'The Lord is my Shepherd'—while driving to Cape Cod in a terrible rainstorm," a man said. Saying it over and over kept him calm and focused while he drove. It helped him to block out the distractions of all the children in the car. It seemed to give him tremendous energies for staying attentive to the road. "After a while," he explained, "the mantra began to say itself." When he arrived, he was actually relaxed and calm, even though tired.

Although some people use standard mantras, such as the Lord's Prayer, the Jesus Prayer, and phrases from the Psalms, you can make up your own mantra. The simpler, the better. Simply choose words and phrases that feel full of spiritual power when you say them. For example, you may use your own name as a centering mantra. As you repeat your name, hear God calling you to be yourself or visualize your fullest self calling you to become all you can become.

The mantra, used by all religions, is one of the most powerful and versatile prayer forms. It is useful for people in all states of mind.

Part II

Prayerways: Feelings and Emotions

Chapter 4

Owning Feelings

To survive and flourish as a spiritual person today, it is important to know what you are feeling, to be able to identify the times you are being moved by feelings and to be able to give names to your feelings, and to know how they affect what you do and how you relate to yourself and others.

Every operation of our bodies, minds, and spirits is permeated by feelings. Many feelings are ordinary and inconsequential; some are special and important. During periods of stress or burnout it is very helpful for people to be able consciously to monitor their feelings and to discern which ones are communicating signals that need to be taken into account.

Recognizing and Owning Your Feelings

The first two steps in becoming conscious that you live in a world of feelings involve recognizing your important feelings and owning them. Step one asks you to say, "I feel such-and-such feelings now." Step two asks you to say, "Yes, those are *my* feelings. They belong to me. I am responsible for them."

But it's not as simple as that. Many of us are not even conscious of our feelings. How often do we find ourselves acknowledging how out of touch with our feelings we are: "I really didn't know how angry I was" or "I didn't realize how disappointed I was" or "It was days later when I realized how devastated and betrayed I had felt." Some of this emotional blindness, our inability to identify and assess the true depth of our feelings, is a healthy protective mechanism. But there are times when we could allow more consciousness of our feelings and consequently react to them on our own behalf.

Take the case of the beleaguered secretary. "Ms. Fredricks, would you mind going by the post office on your way to lunch each day?" was what her boss asked her. Ms. Fredricks took time from her lunch hour to stop at the post office, glad to be helpful. Sometime later, her boss asked, "Ms. Fredricks, we seem to be getting behind. Could you come in for a few hours on Saturdays?" Ms. Fredricks readily agreed and found herself catching up on the work of other people. And soon it became a continuous refrain, "Ms. Fredricks, you wouldn't mind, would you?"

Kind Ms. Fredricks always agreed. She said she didn't mind. She was glad to be helpful. But she did sense some inner whisper of reluctance. Only much later did it occur to her that the boss never asked other workers to come in on Saturdays or to spend their lunch hours standing in a post office line. It was a long time before she was able to acknowledge how she really minded being imposed upon, taken advantage of, and demoralized—how she was slowly burning out as she was burning up with resentment.

Had she been able to get in touch with her inner resistance at the time her boss made his requests, she could have owned her feelings and counteracted the imposing treatment she received by suggesting alternatives like, "I'll do it but I'll probably be late coming back at lunch time, then" or "Let's get everyone to take their turns."

Owning her feelings would have given her the opportunity of growing beyond the seemingly safe place: the sweet, giving person who would never say no, never make anyone feel they were imposing, never hurt anyone's feelings, never make anyone uncomfortable, never turn down a request if it were possible to do, always wear the mask of the "nice" person whom everyone likes.

There is a difference between knowing you have a feeling and owning that feeling. Owning a feeling implies a commitment, taking responsibility for it. I agree to do something about its care. If I own a car, a home, a pet, I have to deal with them, make allowances for them, recognize their needs, make room for them in my life. So it is with owning feelings. They need to be dealt with, cared for, and made room for in one's life.

Parents, for example, can own their feelings toward their children without devastating them. Parents can learn to state their feelings so the children can grow to value the personhood of parents. From their parents' honesty in feelings, children can learn ways for themselves to be emotionally authentic.

Instead, we as parents and grownups often inadvertently encourage children to be emotionally dishonest. By inconsistent behavior we teach children that it is often better to lie or dissemble about how we really feel, even to those who deserve to know our true feelings, sometimes even to ourselves. The message is presented in a variety of ways: "People like you better if you're nice," "It's not nice for little girls to be angry," "You aren't really angry," "Big boys shouldn't be afraid," "You aren't really afraid," "Don't let your father see you pouting," "Be sure you smile for Daddy," or "Just don't let on that it matters and you'll be okay." Each of these statements, in subtle ways, encourages children to be dishonest about their real feelings. Each statement also contains an unspoken promise of reward for hiding unacceptable feelings or threat of rejection for revealing them. Each statement tells children to wear masks over their true feelings.

We don't need to wear "nice people" masks nearly as much as we usually do. Persons with all their complexity of feelings are far more beautiful than any mask, than any work of art.

The Owning Feelings Prayer

In preparing to use the process of owning your feelings in a prayerful way, it is helpful to become aware of—in yourself or others—the wonderful complexity of human personality and feelings. Notice, for example, how seemingly opposing feelings can live together in human beings. See how hate, anger, or dislike don't necessarily wipe out feelings of love. Hate is usually just at the surface, a reaction from anger or disappointment. Notice, for example, how quickly children seem to change in expressing such feelings toward friends and parents. Likewise, even one's deep sadness doesn't wipe out the fundamental joy of life. Recall the laughter and stories of old times that percolate continually during the long hours of an Irish wake!

Perhaps the simplest way to own your feelings prayerfully might be to make lists of your feelings on paper. Listing them forces you to name your feelings. The following four steps may help you:

1. On a piece of paper write down by name every noticeable feeling you've had since awakening this morning. Remember, each feeling is a sign of energy.

2. As you focus on each item, one by one, let yourself acknowledge, "This is indeed a feeling I had or still have. It is *my* feeling. It belongs to me. I own it and I am responsible for dealing with it, for listening to what it has to tell me, and for considering what it asks of me."

3. As you own each feeling, listen to it for any sign of what it has to tell you or ask of you. If something occurs—some word, phrase, image, or connection—make note of it, even if it seems silly or unrelated. For the time being it is not necessary to act on your insight; it is enough to record it.

4. Say thanks to God for each feeling and any related insights you may have had. And let yourself feel grateful for the energies within you that these feelings reveal.

The more precisely you can name your feelings, the easier it is to own them. The larger the number of feelings you are able to identify, the better you are able to appreciate your emotional complexity. The more closely you are able to connect certain feelings with certain people and situations, the sooner you can get to the roots of your burnout and begin to see a way back to full holistic health.

Being Out of Touch with Feelings

For people under heavy stress the basic problem in a prayer involving feelings is that they have probably been long out of touch with many of their true and deep feelings. One challenge in this kind of prayer is to begin to value one's real feelings. This part of the task calls upon me to be able to say that my feelings—even those of despair, loneliness, and unrelatedness—are valuable, are gifts of grace, and can lead me to fuller consciousness of who I am in relation to myself, to others, and to God.

The owning my feelings prayer is basically a prayer of self-awareness. First, it invites me to confront and own my deep feelings. Next, it invites me to see them deeply enough to cooperate with them in their strong urgings toward inner life, to view them not as destructive but instructive. Further, it invites me to see them leading not toward a static and dead homeostasis in my personality but toward a potential dynamic process of growth. This potential calls for one's outer life to be in close harmony with one's inner life, to bring more of the inner world to expression in the outer world, and to observe one's outer world of behavior as a reflection or sign of things happening deep within.

There is a subtlety in feelings—even in strong feelings—that we often miss. My basic anger may have taken on a new twist recently and I didn't notice it; my familiar envy or jealousy may have begun moving in a different direction and I didn't sense it; my childhood fears may have begun expressing themselves with a change in intensity that I haven't measured. In each case recognizing these subtle changes and naming them could be helpfully guiding me to more sensitivity toward myself and others. Psychotherapy is a usual way for people to get in touch with such emotional movements and directions of their personal feelings. The psychotherapeutic process may be described as a relationship that helps put people in touch with their feelings and how these feelings influence their life. Acknowledging one's feelings—anger, sadness, envy, fear, or a host of other strong feelings that can tear fragile human beings apart—also opens the door to healing.

It is important to remember that sometimes burned-out people are afraid that in confronting strong feelings they may consume more energy in dealing with them than they have available. In their desperate desire for peace, in their reaching for a sort of emotional homeostasis, they may be afraid of strong feelings. So they prefer to suppress them, deny them, or project them onto others, thus appearing to be without feelings and without energy.

Typically, burned-out people describe themselves as empty of feelings and empty of energy. "All I need is sleep," they might say. "Let me alone. Let me get some rest."

Unrelatedness and Unrelating

Some burned-out people become so because they are fundamentally unrelated and unrelating. This may seem like a contradiction, since many burnouts happen precisely because the victims are expending themselves for other people. The clue to this type of burnout lies precisely in the *for* other people. Even though burned-out people are usually very busy doing things, they often do not ask to be perceived as persons. They do not invite themselves to be related to as persons, and most often, in a kind of unconscious conspiracy, they do not allow themselves to relate to others as persons. Instead of wanting to be *with* others, they would really rather be *for* them, that is, they prefer not to relate as equals but as unequals, for example, as parents or children, as superiors or servants.

The lack of relatedness may also be manifested in a desire to be alone. While at times a desire to be alone may be very healthy, it is important to get in touch with the kinds of aloneness that deplete a person, the kinds that betray a fundamental unrelatedness. Once such destructive feelings are noticed, they can be called by their true names and owned. Once owned, they can be accepted and something can be done about them. As people start taking steps to change—to recognize themselves as persons and to invite others to recognize them as relating persons—they might ask themselves the following questions:

1. What requests can I make of others that they will begin to see me as a person and not merely as someone who does things for them? How can I put myself back in the world with people in a way that would be energizing rather than draining?
2. Instead of merely wanting to be left alone, can't I turn around and ask of others, "Hey, I want some things from you, too. I want to be recognized as important to you and loveable."
3. How can I find situations to be in where I interact with people in a way that I feel valued, involved, and related to?

To begin taking steps to change, a person might choose to attend classes and to teach something, as a mother of nine children has done in her local community's continuing education program. She teaches a class in art and takes a class in modern dance, "just because it makes me feel good in my body." The dance movements remind her that her body can feel good, and she wants to own those feelings. So this mother, who might be a likely candidate for burnout, has managed to find meaning

and value in what she can share and enjoy with her peers as an
individual person. She is not locked into simply being *for* all
her children.

The Pull Toward Despair

While many burned-out people tend to express themselves as
energyless or unrelated (and unrelatable), there are other
burned-out people who move toward despair. Despair is a dead
end, and the only way out of it is to turn around, to make a
change. The problem is that often such people prefer not to
face their despair and admit it. It seems easier not to have any
feelings. Hope could be the next step if they could take the earlier step, which would be to face the despair and own it.

Despairing people seem to fear hope because hope implies
change, and change seems to demand tremendous energy resources, of which they feel empty. So the vicious circle continues—energylessness to hopelessness to energylessness—unless
they can own their feelings of despair. In this they are like the
alcoholic, the drug addict, or the smoker who can't stop doing
what they know is self-destructive. These victims seem to need
to "hit bottom" and admit it before a change can take place.

Thus when one's burnout is a kind that leads to despair, consciously to be in touch with that feeling of despair is a moment
of grace, a gift. For that moment can be the turning point onto
the road that leads back to the land of the living. Chapter 7
deals more fully with extreme emotions such as despair and
terror.

Feelings and Wholeness

One of the side effects of owning your feelings is a growing
acceptance of the multiplicity of feelings, positive and negative, in yourself and others. You begin to see your own wholeness and the wholeness of others not merely as a set of "nice"
feelings and "nice" behavior but as a deep complexity of feel-

ings that reveals the many faces of your whole life. That holistic insight is a gift to you and one with which you may gift others. It is the gift of valuing your feelings—all of them—enough to let them permeate all your outer life experiences.

Feelings are like pets; you can view them as an enrichment of your life or as a huge burden. How you view feelings depends on your perception of them and how you choose to live with them. You can perceive feelings as a tremendous interference in your life (a very common viewpoint in many spirituality traditions of the past few centuries), or you can choose to live deeply and closely with your feelings as an enrichment of your wholeness. From this perspective every feeling comes with a potential of bringing some richness into your life and some deeper sense of connectedness to the world and to the kingdom.

Feelings are not flaunted, yet they are treasured. They are accounted for and kept alive as part of the inheritance to be passed on to those who come in touch with you—family, friends, and colleagues. Your strong feelings touch the world indelibly; they are part of your bequest to the evolving world, in your lifetime as well as when you die.

In this sense owning your feelings in prayer is an experience of connectedness. Through the vitality of your emotions and feelings you are connected to yourself, to your story, to other humans, and to the whole planet as it evolves into the kingdom of God.

Chapter 5

Drawing Feelings

While owning your feelings allows you to put your emotions into words, the next step allows you to express your feelings in images, colors, and shapes, which can often reach beyond the written or spoken word. It is helpful to take this next step—the imaginative representation of feelings—because feelings usually seem to enter consciousness connected to some representation. One person connects anger to a visit from in-laws, another with rush-hour traffic, a third to delays at work, another to a child's messy room. Ask people what image comes to mind when they think of anger and their answers will probably include concrete images or representations.

Every feeling has one or more dynamic images connected with it. To name a feeling is to begin to get in touch with the imagery associated with it.

Feelings represent values as well as energy. Therefore feelings help identify the important moments of your life. Events connected with your strongest feelings are probably the major scenes of your life story. That is why when feelings seem to cease, as in times of stress or burnout, one's life seems at an end and meaningless. To lose contact with your feelings is to lose contact with your life story and your meaning.

In this loss occurs also the loss of imagery, the loss of those representations of people, places, and things that symbolize feelings. Therefore, especially in time of burnout, it is essential to remain in touch with your feelings and the images connected with them.

Though drawing feelings may not have been associated with traditional spirituality, the activity has been used therapeutically for many decades. Here we introduce the activity of drawing as a healing mode of prayer.

Steps of the Prayer

While there are a variety of ways to make the connection between drawing and prayer, most of the ways seem to proceed through a few common steps, as follows:

1. Get in touch with a feelings state. It may be a feeling remembered, brought to life again through imagination, or one that is strong in you this very moment.
2. Using pencil, pen, crayons, felt markers, brushes, or your fingers, spontaneously express your feeling state, recognized or remembered, in shapes, images, and colors. Work as rapidly or as reflectively as is comfortable for you. Have no concern for technical skill. Turn off your rational mind and just let the drawing flow. Do not expect it to make sense.
3. When your drawing seems complete, thank God for the opportunity of letting your hand express your feelings. Reaffirm that your feelings and your images reveal that energy does indeed flow in you.

Some people like to hang their drawings in places they are likely to notice the images frequently. As they make new drawings, they may hang them up alongside earlier ones. If any insight should happen after a number of drawings, make note of it somewhere and give gratitude to the spirit who inspired it.

Getting Started

For those who resist drawing at any time or who seem to have difficulty getting into the process, here are a few suggestions.

One approach is to blindfold yourself and then begin to draw. Another catalyst is music that seems to reflect your current emotional state; then simply draw what the music seems to be communicating.

A third suggestion—a technique often used by art therapists—is to draw a house, a tree, and a person. Technical drawing skill seems to be unimportant in effectively using this technique. Each element of your drawing can reveal much about yourself. The house can reflect, for example, how you see yourself in the larger world, how you welcome the world, the face you present to it, or your view of your body and general appearance. For example, is your house hidden, withdrawn, dark, very insignificant, off to the side, windowless, or doorless? Or is it attractive, open, welcoming, cheerful, mysterious, sturdy, and full of light and warmth?

The tree can reflect the more primitive and nature-connected parts of your personality, how you feel in your environment, how you respond to nature and instincts within you. For example, is your tree tall, strong, proud, deeply rooted, wide branched, and full of leaves? Or is it weak, stunted, branchless, thin, and without roots?

The person in your drawing can express how you relate to people. For example, is your person small, hidden, sad, immobile, afraid, without hands and fingers, and without ears or hair? Or is your person smiling, attractive, reaching out, touching things, open-eyed, rich in detail, and healthy? Reflection on your house-tree-person drawing can provide material for prayers.

Over time, as various psychological and spiritual changes take place in you, they will probably be reflected in the elements of your drawing.

A fourth way to help you get into drawing your feelings was suggested by a woman who wrote a poem about her strong feelings and at the end of the poem found herself doing a drawing. Begin this process with a verbal-symbolic description of your feelings, as in a poem, and move into a pictorial-symbolic depiction of them. The woman explained how the drawing allowed her to affirm a level of feelings beyond what she was able to state in words. It was as if words were not as powerful as the images—an island in a stormy sea, one sailboat in the sea, one tall tree alone being blown in a storm, one huge eye in a sky, half storm and half sun-filled, with raindrops for its tears. Her poem pointed the way to an understanding of the images in her drawing and allowed her to become conscious of the work she had to do in terms of her own identity, finding out who she was in contrast to the self who always tried to meet other people's expectations of her.

What she had denied herself in terms of knowing herself had come out in the poem. To be whole she would have to allow out parts of herself that were not quite socially welcome. The poem spoke of her wanting to weep the unshed tears that grieved the absence of her total self for many years. The drawing—the lonely island, the solitary sailboat, the tree alone—revealed her sense of loneliness in stepping out into this new world alone. The storms and winds emphasized her inner storms, the conflicting elements in her grief. The boat and tree looked graceful but were being whipped by the winds. She had a sense that the ocean could in a moment overwhelm the island—her tiny new emerging total self. But there was a sun and a big, mystical eye. The eye might be sad, but its tears gave release. Finally, she realized nothing in her drawing indicated the tree or sailboat couldn't tolerate the storm. The drawing seemed to be a statement from her inner self that the deeper parts of her human nature—the unconscious seas and the unpredictable storms—were doing a lot of stirring around at the present time.

A fifth way to enter the drawing would be to tell a story—

speak it aloud—as you draw. The characters or figures in your drawing can't move or talk on the paper, but you can give them life and the ability to speak by creating a story to accompany your drawing. One frightened child was unable to tell a story as he drew his picture, but he was able to sing a story in the manner of a medieval ballad.

A sixth way to begin is to use a mandala framework. Draw a circle that almost completely fills your blank piece of paper. Then close your eyes and let yourself relax. Music in the background helps. Let a box of colored crayons sit in front of you. When you feel ready, reach for a color you want to use. Don't think about what you are going to draw, just be aware of your hand reaching out for the crayon it wants. Then let your hand dictate the motion of the lines and shapes you draw. If images you feel you would like to draw within the circle come to mind, draw them. Feel free to change your images or to change the colors you use. Let colors represent your feelings; let the pressure with which you draw represent the intensity of your feelings; let your hands draw in the circle the feelings that are currently at the center of your life.

One man in a psychotherapeutic group of eight people drew eight flowers in his mandala circle. "I want to bloom in our group," he explained, pointing to one flower. "I want all of us to bloom," he added, pointing to all the flowers. "I want us to have the experience of blooming together." That was his prayer.

A seventh way is to draw yourself and how you feel right now, not a picture of your physical appearance but of how you feel about yourself, the images you have of yourself on a feeling level. A woman in graduate school drew herself with a hat over her head. What was unique about the drawing was that the hat was enormous, covering more than half the drawing paper. How appropriate for a graduate student preoccupied with developing her mind. Another woman drew herself with a baby's face, a mother's apron on, and a seductive feminine body: she was mother, child, and seductress all in one.

An eighth way is to draw yourself as you think God sees you.

A ninth way is to do comparison drawings: the first, the way you picture yourself in a state of burnout and the second, the way you would like to be, full of energy. Compare the two drawings. Where on the burnout body are the energies lacking? What do these energies look like—make them colorful— on the energized body? As an additional stage in this prayer process, try to stand like and feel like the energized person. Express in your body the face in that energized drawing, its body posture, its inner spirit. Tell yourself you want to actualize the energized drawing.

Drawings of the energized body are very fascinating to do. Psychoeducator Paula Klimek asked a group of fifth graders to draw their energized bodies. A child would lie down on a six-foot strip of butcher paper and Paula would trace the body's outline in black. For the next few weeks the children drew with colored felt markers the way they perceived their own energy systems, their own strengths and weaknesses operating inside and outside their body's boundaries. The drawings were a startling revelation of the depth of self-awareness each child had, for they spoke excitedly about the meaning of the colors and energies they had drawn.

The Prayer Experience

"But," some people might ask, "where is the prayer experience in all these procedures?" In one sense, the drawing itself is a prayer experience, for even though one is not carrying on a verbal dialogue with God, one is getting in touch with the ultimate sources of life within oneself. It is to raise one's mind and heart to things connected to God. To become consciously aware of life in feelings is to make contact with God at work within us.

In order more consciously to make this experience an act of relating to God, you might wish to begin your drawing time by focusing your attention on God's presence in your life, expressing your gratitude for the gift of feelings and emotions, and asking that the exploration of your feelings help bring about your own growth and hasten the advent of God's kingdom in your life and in the world.

Also you may bring a drawing-your-feelings experience to a close with a few moments of formal prayer, during which you may, for example, praise or thank God for the gift of life, express your sorrow for having missed or wasted certain life energies, or petition God for more energy.

A short after-prayer reflection time will almost always prove valuable in assessing insights into your self and the feelings that happened during the prayer time. Such insights or awareness are gifts given to us by God to help us transform our lives. Self-transformation, the final step in the prayer process, is basically a task for the conscious mind and the conscious will. While prayer usually generates insights, the active will is the personal faculty that translates these insights into action and makes them real in the world.

Chapter 6

Dialoguing with Feelings

Dialoguing with feelings moves us to a third step, deeper into an awareness of the dynamic power of feelings. In the first step we named and owned our feelings; in the second step by drawing our feelings we symbolized them in images and connected them to our life story. In this third step we allow the feelings *to reply*, to describe our situation from their viewpoint, to challenge us, and to speak up on behalf of the inner self. Dialoguing means exactly what it says: to hold a conversation.

Preparing for Dialogue

Before we can hold a conversation with our feelings, we should probably take a few preparatory steps. First of all, identify and name the feeling with which you want to dialogue. Name it as precisely as you can. Is it anger, anxiety, fear, anticipation, sadness, melancholy, wistfulness, loneliness, exhaustion, frustration, boredom, discouragement, despair, grief, joy, astonishment, or hope?

Second, once you've given the feeling a first name, also give it a last name if you can; that is, identify the parent or source of the feeling. Who or what sired the feeling in you? For example, if anxiety is the name of the feeling and the anxiety comes from losing a job, then you might dialogue with Anxiety Job. If the anxiety comes from moving from Riverview, then you might dialogue with Anxiety Riverview. Uncle Sam is a good example of how we personify and name an abstract system like the government, a corporation, or the church.

If the feeling with which you want to dialogue is anger, specify by name the situation that helped generate the angry feelings in you. Perhaps it was your spouse, your ex-boss, a professor, a friend, or yourself (for example, for failing an exam). In each case, give your anger a last name so that when you dialogue with the feeling, you can call it by its full name. Somehow we can put more intensity into a full name than a single name. As an angry Liza Doolittle sang in *My Fair Lady*, "Just you wait, Henry Higgins, just you wait!" Being able to snarl and hiss the "Higgins" made a lot of difference in becoming aware of how strong her anger really was.

Third, begin the dialogue by imagining the feeling quite like another person or being standing or sitting opposite you, able to hear your words and reply to them. Some people like to sit or stand opposite an empty chair, visualizing the feeling personified and sitting in the empty chair. Others prefer to imagine the personified feeling sitting inside their mind, talking to them by a kind of mental telepathy.

Fourth, many people find it helpful to write down the dialogue as they hear it. In this way they preserve a written record of the dialogue. If future dialogues happen and are written down, an evolving history of interaction with this feeling may be kept and reflected upon. Such written dialogues may be shared with a counselor or spiritual director. You can make a pact with yourself to read over your dialogues after a certain period of time. It is often surprising how new levels of insight can arise from rereadings.

Approaching the Dialogue

At the beginning of any dialogue session ask God to be present and to bless you and the feelings with which you are about to dialogue.

The first approach focuses on the present, the here and now of the feeling. When you have personified the feeling, perhaps giving it the shape of a human, an animal, a plant, or an object, then you address the feeling, calling it by name and asking it the following questions: "Why are you in my life?" "Why are you here right now?" "What have you to teach me?" "How can I help you?" Wait for an answer. If you are writing the dialogue, write down your question and the character's answer. Don't be in a hurry to go to a second question until you have heard everything the feeling character has to say about the first question.

Even if an answer appears to make no sense, write it down exactly as you seem to hear it. If other clarifying questions occur to you as the character talks, by all means ask them. Some characters will answer your questions in a straightforward manner; others will reply in symbolic and paradoxical ways. Usually, an uncomfortable or seemingly destructive feeling will not leave you until you have learned what it has to teach you and/or have given it whatever kind of help, support, or recognition it demands from you.

A second approach to dialoguing with feelings focuses on the past, the historical or psychological origins of a feeling. In this approach you address a feeling character by name and ask one or other of the following questions, which will allow you to trace the feeling back to its roots in your life: "Where were you conceived?" "With what other people in my family and life do you have a history?" "When did you first come to life in me?" "How did you grow into the position you now have in my life?"

Here, too, writing down the questions and replies helps bring the psychospiritual dynamic of this procedure into greater consciousness, especially for the burnout victim who needs to deal with the roots of certain destructive feelings. Writing helps articulate and clarify. Actual words and expressions from the feeling character can be coming from the wisdom of the unconscious spirit, surfacing at this special prayer moment in order to give important guidance signs.

Some people find their characters give their best insights in puns and slips of the tongue. For example, a woman reported she represented her feelings of confusion in the character of a lovely biracial child, who answered the question, "What have you to teach me?" by replying, "Look at me right in the I." In this pun the woman recognized her own need to acknowledge both the acceptable and unacceptable parts of herself, to acknowledge and be open to the biracial child within her.

It is very significant in dealing with strong feelings to get in touch with their roots. Roots include old attitudes and feelings you carry with you and unconsciously bring into your new relationships and new places.

A man who carried an attitude of self-sufficiency with him for decades always came into relationships prepared to do all the work, to assume full responsibility not only for getting his own needs met but for making each relationship work. He was one of those people who cannot let anyone do anything for him. "I can do it by myself" was his unspoken motto. Consequently, none of his relationships ever felt successful because he would never agree to be equals. He always needed to maintain control, to be the one responsible for everything. Once he became conscious of this pattern, he wanted to let go of it. He wanted to be more open, more vulnerable, to share the responsibility of making a relationship succeed. Dialoguing with the roots of his self-sufficiency feeling enabled him to make peace with it, and while keeping it strong in certain areas, he learned to ask it to stay out of his friendships.

A third approach to interacting with a feeling character is to carry it forward, perhaps into the future. In this approach some typical questions to ask your feeling character might be "What will happen if I keep you?" "What will happen if I allow you to grow and expand?" "What part do you want to play in my life?" "What will happen to me if I let go of you?" Let your imagination explore its way into the coming hours, days, or years of your life. See how the feeling, which has come up through your roots, will branch out as you move forward.

A working mother had growing feelings of frustration and anger at her teenage children. She named her feeling character Frustration Children and pictured it as a scowling face with a big mouth, pointed teeth, and a long, blood-red tongue.

"Frustration Children," she began, "my four kids are in the family room watching television while I'm doing dishes alone. They never volunteer to help; they don't cooperate; they don't clean up their rooms. I feel angry, frustrated, and unappreciated. What will happen if I allow you to express yourself to them?" "How would you use me?" the character asked in reply. "I would stomp into the family room and snap off the television set," she replied. "I would angrily tell them about my sense of being tired and unappreciated. I would tell them that I felt they were lazy and uncooperative, that all they did was take and never give, leaving me feeling drained. And I would probably demand that they come to the kitchen immediately and help me with the dinner dishes."

"The best I can do with that," said Frustration Children, "is probably to get the dishes done. But there wouldn't be any love in their dishwashing. You'd have released me—your anger and frustration—on them, but I can't produce feelings of appreciation for you or cooperation in them. More than likely I'll produce confusion in them, which might make them say, 'How come Mom never reacted like this before? We've been watching TV after dinner since as long as we can remember, and she never said a word. Something must be wrong.'"

"Okay," she replied, "I don't want to use you that way. What if after the dishes are done and TV time is over I sit the kids down and tell them of my angry feelings and what I was thinking of doing, but didn't do?"

"I don't want to be in your life," interrupted Frustration Children, "if all you want me for is to get your tomorrow's dishes cleaned. That's not a good use of my time and energy. It seems your problem is with your relationship to your kids. Haven't you got any other strong feelings to talk to about them besides me?" "Well, yes. I'd really like to spend more time with them, and I wish we could have some fun together and be close." "Sounds like fun and closeness feelings could help you better than I can."

With that the angry feelings left her. And it occurred to her that there was another alternative. She could leave the dishes in the sink, go into the family room, and say, "I'd like to watch television and be with you." And she would add, as an unimportant afterthought, "Afterwards, we can all go to the kitchen and do the dishes."

Each of the prayerways related to feelings calls you to choose to be alive as fully as you can. At times this means you may have to choose to feel alive, even in the emotional pain of anger, failure, and loss. Pain is a sign of life wanting to be expressed. In each case, when the prayer experience comes to a resolution or to some natural stopping place, come back into your ordinary consciousness and, after thanking God, spend some minutes reflecting on what you learned. Paradoxically, in your pain, your problems, and your woundedness may be found your unique path to wholeness and to holiness.

Chapter 7

Despair and Terror

Hiding Despair

Discouragement, failure, despair, and dread feel like the end of the line. We wish we could simply die and not have to keep on trying. How many of us feel it yet deny it? In an age of anxiety we grow adept at sweeping it under the rug and putting on a "life is fine" face.

The despair we feel is not only a personal burden; there is also a despair that belongs to us as a people. We hear the signals of distress—nuclear threats, the end of fossil fuels, the shredding of the social fabric—all around us; and yet these social and global alarms, paradoxically, usually receive only public apathy. The dread of what might happen in the near future is pushed out to the fringes of awareness. Yet it is there, waiting offstage—frightful and fearful despair.

The more we suppress seemingly ultimate feelings like dread and despair, the more numbed our sensitivities grow, the more apathetic and dead we seem to become. In such denial and suppression we potentially deny and suppress our own life energies.

It takes tremendous energy to keep despair under wraps. The hiding process consumes energy that would otherwise be used creatively to find alternatives, seek a fresh vision, or process important information. Instead, loving loses its luster, nature loses its wonder, other people become less real and uninteresting, and living becomes a burden.

Joanna Rogers Macy states, "Despair cannot be banished by sermons on positive thinking' or injections of optimism. Like grief, it must be worked through. It must be named and validated as a healthy, normal, human response to the planetary situation. Faced and experienced, despair can be *used*: as the psyche's defenses drop away, new energies are released."*

Facing Despair

To face distress and despair openly and clearly is the first step in the dynamics of working through despair: to be willing to unleash what happens when you allow yourself to acknowledge, name, and feel the inner pain of despair.

Despair may be defined as the loss of the assumption that you (or the human species) will ever pull through. It is awareness of the possibility that the "experiment" that is you (or the planet) may fail.

People who try to hide their despair, especially when they are growing conscious of it, often experience onslaughts of deep sadness that happen at unexplainable times: when they look at a certain photo, hear the melody of a special song, or see the words of a familiar poem. Others report physical symptoms: a sense of heavy weights on the chest, cold sweats, violent shaking, or an impulse to hide or to lie in the fetal posture. Many experience suicidal fantasies and/or death wishes.

Facing despair will also usually demand that you experience a loss of control and a sense of powerlessness. Spiritually, despair may be experienced as a loss of faith and hope. One's religious support system seems not to work at all. God seems to have left the scene completely. Socially, despairing persons are faced with a dilemma. There seems to be no one they want to turn to. Even if there are compassionate friends and family, Jo-

* Joanna Rogers Macy, "How to Deal with Despair," *New Age* (June 1979), p. 41.

anna Rogers Macy says, "Do I want them to feel this horror, too?" Besides, what can anyone *say*?

Social activists, whose despair is not only a personal thing but is connected with events in society as well, find few people among spiritual counselors and psychotherapists who can fully understand the many dimensions of their pain. They grieve not only for themselves but for all the unseen and unborn suffering that is happening and will surely continue to happen. Acknowledging despair, like faith, calls us to let go of the assumption that I and we can fully control events.

Signs of Hope and Wholeness

To experience pain and anxiety in the face of much destruction and suffering is a healthy thing, whether the destruction is happening to you or to somebody else. What is unhealthy is to suppress the pain and anxiety.

Although it seems if we unleash the forces of despair in ourselves, we will go to pieces, perhaps such an event is one of the special pathways to hope and wholeness. If despair is kind enough to take all the pieces of us apart, then those pieces are in readiness to be rebuilt into a new and different system. Of course, it's difficult to operate as a normal, healthy human being when one's pieces are, so to speak, spread out all over the place. Spiritually, at a time like this one feels dismembered, in a spiritual void, and utterly vulnerable. But this time of anxieties and doubts is essentially a healthy and creative time because it is a time that permits a new thrust toward the real person who can be shaped from all those spread out parts.

What disintegrates and gets spread all over is not our essential self or soul but the ideals, values, defenses, and attitudes that gave visible and social shape to our inner core. Some of them are no longer most appropriate for our further growth. Perhaps they restrict our vision, block the flow of information, make it harder for us to see and to adapt, or standardize our responses.

Experiencing our despair with feelings of pain is a sign we are alive. The pain tells us there is a deeper feeling beneath the despair still awaiting resurrection: that is our power to love. Our anguish in despair is rooted in compassion and caring for ourselves and others. To drop our defenses and let the grief surface brings release of the pain and reveals our connection to each other.

Even in the depths of despair, when we often hear ourselves ask the question, "What is real and what isn't?" we realize our capacity for love and caring is very real. It is the nature of love to extend and expand itself. Its goal is peace and unity, within oneself and with others; its way of operating is through compassion and practicing forgiveness, toward oneself and toward others. Psychiatrist Gerald Jampolsky often suggests to the extremely ill children with whom he works that, since only love is real, they always put themselves in a position to help another person, no matter how badly off they think they are.

Praying in Times of Despair

Joanna Macy suggests a breathing meditation that involves giving yourself permission to experience your suffering or the sufferings of others, using the imagination to visualize the sufferer as vividly as possible.

Next the sufferings, like a stream of dark air, are inhaled with the breath and drawn into the heart and through it. The sufferings are meant to be felt in the heart, the seat of caring and compassion in the human being.

You are not asked to do anything for your despair or the despair of others; you are asked only to experience it. And wait. Actively.

One opposite of waiting is to act impetuously, thoughtlessly, to short-circuit the healing process, to try to force it. Another opposite of waiting—active waiting—is apathy, to close one's eyes and ears, to shut off all life systems, and to cast off any responsibility for what one does or for what happens to others. True waiting, in contrast, is done with open eyes, open ears, and open heart. Everything in one is alive—painfully so—watching for possibilities.

Another way to pray in time of despair is to get rid of the "fearful child" parts of yourself. These parts include those fears, guilts, judgments, expectations, and unwarranted assumptions of responsibility that increase the oppressiveness of your despair. Once these parts are collected, they may be placed, using your imagination, in a box—one by one. Do this action as consciously, as vividly, and as concretely as possible.

Then, as your imagination suggests, you may tie the box to a helium-filled balloon and let it get carried away; you may tie the box to a heavy stone and drop it in a lake; or you may burn the box until its contents become charred embers no longer having any power over you at all.

One woman wrote on slips of paper each of the elements of her life that contributed to her growing despair. As she put each slip in the special box she had set aside for this purpose, she asked God for the strength to let go of this fearful part of herself. In the end she ceremonially burned the box with all the fear slips in it, seeing the smoke symbolizing all her fears rising to heaven for God's acceptance.

Praying in Time of Terror

Terror is defined as fear so strong it cripples the fearful person physically, mentally, and spiritually. Working through extreme feelings such as terror, despair, and grief involves a similar process; all three require the person to be willing to acknowledge the feeling and to be willing to experience the pain of it fully and openly.

While working through grief involves acceptance of a loss that has occurred, working through terror usually involves a "loss" that has not yet occurred, and its "acceptance" usually provokes a most violent reaction. In the dynamic of terror, it is precisely the unknown elements of the terror experience that figure most prominently in it.

Terror differs from despair, as well as from grief. In despair the body, mind, and spirit tend to plummet downward toward inaction and depression, where to do anything—even the simplest daily tasks—requires extreme effort and seems to exhaust one's entire energies. In contrast, terror usually heightens all responses. Terrified people want to run, scream, beat their fists, tear out their hair; they want to be held and protected; their minds run anxiously and wildly in a thousand directions, usually aimlessly. Energy is pouring out every pore of their body, uncontrollably.

Using Mantras

Hence, prayer during times of terror and high anxiety can seldom follow a disciplined procedure, especially when the terror is at a critical point. Usually the best that can be hoped for are scattered moments of awareness when a very short mantra prayer might be begun and continued for some seconds until awareness is lost again. Such a prayer often takes the form of an utterly simple exclamation, such as "Jesus!" or "God!" or "God help me!" or "Lord, have mercy!" Forms of divine supplication learned in childhood can also be helpful here, for at these times we are very close to our childlike feelings of helplessness in terrors and nightmares. A mother responding to a terrified child often repeats soothing words and uses rhythmic stroking or rocking. Therefore it helps if terrified persons can do something further to involve their body: screaming, groaning, wailing, sobbing, rolling on the floor, jumping up and down, or flapping their arms—releasing the anxiety-generated energy in any way possible. One man said that in times of terror he hugged his stomach, rocked his body, and murmured the plea "Please, God" again and again.

Getting Centered

If at all possible, the terror-stricken person should stop for a few two-minute periods during the day to breathe slowly through the diaphragm: inhaling to a count of 1-2-3, holding the breath to a count of 1-2-3, then expelling the breath to a count of 1-2-3. (Instead of counting 1-2-3, the person may recite a mantra three times.) During inhaling, visualize, if possible, the white light of God's energy entering and transforming you; during exhaling, visualize the terror being expelled with your breath.

This is a very simple centering procedure and will be most helpful if used frequently and regularly during the day. Physically, the procedure is known to help slow the heartbeat and reduce blood pressure; psychologically, it allows people to "get hold" of themselves; spiritually, it opens the channels for special gifts of spiritual energy.

Terror, despair, and grief are not experiences to be gotten over in a short time. These traumatic experiences leave much turbulence in their wake, and people should not be surprised to feel their effects weeks, months, even years later. They are extremely significant life events and need to be worked through thoroughly on the physical, psychological, and spiritual levels. It is outside the scope of this book to explain that process. In general, however, overwhelming feelings do need to be worked through, and part of that work involves the willingness to acknowledge, feel, and express the inner pain involved. The modes of prayer related to owning, drawing, and dialoguing with feelings should prove helpful in the long process of working through grief, terror, and despair.

Part III

Prayerways: The Reflective Mind

Chapter 8

One Step at a Time

June's brother had died a short time ago and tonight she and her husband were driving home after just having registered her father-in-law in a nursing home. With these two big troubles in their hearts and with rain beating on their windshield, June and her husband, both exhausted, planned to have a light supper at home and go to bed early.

As they pulled into their driveway, they sensed something was wrong. Moments later they discovered their house had been broken into while they were away. Their front door had been smashed in, and glass and splinters were strewn all over their front hall.

June and her husband wept and hugged each other; anger, fear, hurt, and exhaustion flowed through them. Finally, he said, "One step at a time, June. Let's just take it one step at a time." They were then able to name what needed to be done and to set about doing it.

Afterwards June said, "My one comfort was that misfortune comes in threes, and after my brother and my father-in-law, this was number three." June recognized that while the break-in was not welcome, it was not overwhelming. It was something she and her husband could handle if they handled it one step at a time.

When life collapses, you can rebuild it if you do it step by step. When facing a seemingly insurmountable problem, you can divide and conquer. Problems are usually made up of little pieces. You can clarify the pieces and do one thing at a time.

Are you moving into a new home or apartment where the place is a mess? Are you transferring into a new job where you feel overwhelmed and inadequate? Are you facing the responsibility of a decision where you feel you've gotten yourself in over your head? Are you involved in a project that makes you feel tired even before you begin? In each kind of situation like these, the one step at a time prayer seems helpful.

Doing the Prayer

1. Begin the process by getting in touch with your problem and with your goal or needs (what you want to achieve). Usually when people can say clearly what they want in a situation, they can explore the steps they need to take in order to bring about their desired outcome.

2. Try to write out each step that must be taken in order to achieve what you desire. Make your steps simple and easy. Don't try to skip steps, to leap ahead, or to get there by a clever detour. This is a lesson—don't try to skip steps—that every sick person learns in making his or her way back to health and that every parent learns in helping a sick child back to health.

3. As you perform each step, offer it consciously to God *as one more step* in the process of achieving what needs to be done. As you make decisions or do things one by one, lay them to rest as they are made. Tell God you have done your best in the circumstances and then proceed to the next step.

One burnout victim found it overwhelming to think of having to write twenty-five Christmas cards. When asked if she could write one card today and one tomorrow, she said yes. So she wrote one each day until they were all done.

A special part of the one step at a time prayer is to ask

"Whom can I get to help me?" For example, in the many details of dealing with birth, death, marriage, moving, or changing jobs—making arrangements, contacting people, and so forth—give other people a chance to help you. Let them help you with decisions, organization, details, performance, and support, especially when you feel you may not have the energy by yourself to do all that has to be done.

A good suggestion in doing the one step at a time prayer is to remember to let your first step be something of which you're sure you're capable. Teachers of children with severe learning disabilities begin with tasks such children are sure to succeed in performing, and from these first sure steps they move patiently and evenly forward.

Remedial Spiritual Development

This suggestion is also applicable to people who need to do remedial work in spiritual development. At times, for example, adults want to reconnect with their spiritual values. Some of these people had left off their conscious spiritual growth at age six or seven, "where we were told that our guardian angel took care of all our needs," explained a mature physicist. "But at fifty years old the guardian angel theory doesn't really satisfy."

How do people catch up spiritually to where they have emotionally and intellectually grown? Learning from the remedial teachers, the best way to begin is to go back in your spiritual history to a time when you were on sure ground and then grow step by step toward today.

To get in touch with your spiritual history, you may want to write out your early remembered moments of prayer: at your bedside, hiding somewhere, in the midst of nature, kneeling in church. Trace your history of prayer, the history of how you wanted to be cared for by God, when and how you asked for that caring.

From the steps you have experienced, slowly move to exploring other ways of relating to God. As you have grown older, you have loved and cared for others and you have grown to know what it means to be loved. Recall your original way of praying and try it again: tell God who you are and what you want. Then integrate your own maturity into the experience. One man explained it this way:

> When I was a child, when I related and when I prayed, I did all the talking. Now that I'm older, I have discovered in my relationships that I want not only to talk but to listen. So in my prayers I began to listen to God as well as to talk. As a child, too, I felt there was only one way to have my prayers answered. As a man, I have learned there are many different answers to a request. As a child, I also believed that the present moment was the only moment there was, and I had to have things done for me instantly. Now I begin to see my life as a process and this day as only one moment in that long process.

This man learned that he did not need to discard his childhood faith and spiritual patterns, but simply enriched and expanded them through the experience of his life. He now listened to the inner movements of God's spirit in his life; he learned to look in many places for answer to his prayers; and he discovered that God's caring is for our total life rather than for a momentary wish and that one's total life journey is made up of many single steps.

Chapter 9

Journal of Blessings

Once at a home sabbath service the rabbi invited the small congregation to prepare for their worship with a fifteen-minute quiet reflection on blessings received during the past week. People were asked, beginning with the last sabbath, to spend two minutes per day recalling significant moments of each day.

After the meditation, people mentioned to the group some of their remembered moments of blessing. They shared gratitude for health and recovery from sickness, for success in business or school, for awarenesses about nature and God, for new discoveries about themselves, for mended relationships, and for unexpected pleasures or surprises.

Although preparation for the formal sabbath service had taken half an hour, it was well worth it for all of the congregation approached the sabbath prayer with hearts very consciously and concretely full of gratitude. The rabbi's meditation had the same purpose as keeping a journal of blessings.

Keeping a Journal

To keep a journal, it is helpful to have a little notebook to hold a day-to-day record of the blessings you notice. Using the book helps you concretize your blessings and keeps a permanent record of them. What should you write down in your journal of blessings? Write down anything—no matter how seemingly insignificant—that happened and *made you feel good about yourself.*

If you are in the midst of burnout, you may not think that there is anything that can make you feel good about yourself. As one person put it, "There's a feeling of sameness about everything when you're in burnout. One day goes on after the other, and they're all boring. There are no dynamics in life. It goes on in a blur."

Another person described the burnout experience not in terms of boredom but in terms of tiredness. "Burnout to me feels like a time of extreme tiredness, when I feel I'm being taken for granted and I don't care 'cause I'm taking everything for granted, too. I'm not doing much and I can't see much happening in the world. Besides, I haven't got the energy to do anything."

The journal can help you get past a sense of tiredness or sameness and bring some bits of vividness into your life, so moments of your day become meaningful and feel like more than just the passage of time.

Which Blessings to Count

Begin noting very simple experiences that make you feel good about yourself. Start with your morning ritual—a refreshing shower, a good breakfast, a hot cup of coffee or tea, and whatever else you enjoy about the morning: sunshine outdoors, the car starting up the first time you turn on the ignition, catching the bus or train, getting the children off smoothly, a pleasant memory, thought, or encounter, a few quiet moments to yourself, and so on.

During your day learn to watch for the little blessings that people tend to overlook: buying a piece of clothing on a special sale, finding a dollar bill in your pants just before you throw them in the clothes washer; discovering some item you thought you had lost; enjoying a book or magazine; finding something interesting in a newspaper; rediscovering a favorite photo, poem, recipe, piece of music; remembering your mother's birthday this year; walking in the rain deliberately; taking a hot bath; finding a time and a place to cry; hearing someone say to you, "I love you"; having somebody kiss you by surprise; or receiving a warm hug, handshake, and so on.

If you come to the end of a day and there are only a few items on your blessings list, then that's a time for doing something nice for yourself. Treat yourself to something that will make you feel good about yourself. Take time to sit down and play music, take a shower and sing some favorite songs, or give yourself a foot bath and a pedicure or a foot massage. Let your own creativity suggest things that would be blessings for you. Above all, let yourself enjoy the blessing you are taking the time to do. Then make note of it in your blessings journal.

If you use a very small notebook for your journal, you can carry it in your pocket or purse so that when a small blessing happens to you, you can immediately write down a word or two about the experience. At night read over your notes and say a word of thanks to God for each of the blessings you received—those you noted and those you didn't. In this way you begin to use your journal as a prelude to prayer. At the end of the week look back over your notebook at the blessings that happened during the week and thank God once again for them.

Alternatives

Besides listing the small and large blessings that come to you day by day, there are many other blessings you might note. One alternative (or additional) way to realize your blessings would be to *list all the things you like to do*. This list might include items like going to plays, going to movies, going to art galleries, going to museums, going out to dinner, taking a drive in a car, attending workshops, taking walks, ice-skating, dancing, playing chess, discussing early American history, cooking, or planning parties. Next to each item you might like to put the names of all the people you know who also like to do these things and/or might like to do them with you. Listing names of people will remind you of all the potential connections with people that await you in your life.

A second alternative is to *list your friends and acquaintances.* List the people in your life and what they bring—actually or potentially—into a relationship with you. Here again is emphasized the tremendous potential that exists among people.

A third alternative is to *list things that happened in your life that have made you feel good in the past* or make you feel good whenever they happen: breakfast in bed, nice music, a good book, a shampoo, or a television comedy.

A fourth alternative is to *list the blessings that came to you during childhood.* After you make such a list—at least twenty-five items—check to see which of these blessings are still coming to you in some form and which have ceased. Among those that have ceased are there any that you would like to restore? If so, how might you go about getting them restored?

A fifth alternative is to *list your personal interests, talents, skills, and resources.* Among your gifts you might include being a good listener, clean-up person, bridge player, laugher, storyteller, lover, cook, or worker.

We need not be afraid to affirm ourselves. God loves us unconditionally and blesses us with our lives and with an invitation to participate in divine life. If God is willing and eager to affirm us so powerfully, how natural and right it must be for us to acknowledge that value and lovableness that is God's gift to us.

Chapter 10

List of My Wants

A California physician has each of his new patients make a list of ten things they really want to do in life, especially those patients who suffer from such maladies as asthma, ulcer, colitis, hypertension, and depression. Their wants may be to take piano lessons, to start painting, to begin writing a book, or to arrange for that long-denied trip to Europe. At the end of their visit the physician assigns the first want on the list: "Begin doing what you have written here as your number one want."

By inviting people to live out some of their cherished wants, this physician has found a simple way to help people discover hidden energies that often have a power to heal that his medicines do not possess. Getting in touch with one's wants often helps getting in touch with one's latent energies. As wants begin getting translated into reality, people begin to discover their energies.

Some Difficulties

Some people have difficulty getting in touch with their wants. One college student said she got stuck trying to think of a single want. This young woman, it turned out, spent her whole life trying to be supergood, superkind, and super-thoughtful. She was tied into the psychological game of "not living unless you live perfectly." She wouldn't allow her weaknesses to live, nor would she let her wants live. She finally expressed her wants, saying, "It seems crazy, but when I think of the things I want, there is only one: I want to live." If you feel stuck, as this student did, try at least to get in touch with *one* want.

Some people have difficulty getting started with their wants list. A law student who arrived for a first counseling visit dressed in a very traditional lawyer's three-piece suit, said he hadn't many wants. He sat up very straight in the chair, made very little eye contact, and came on as an intellectual, proud of himself and with a streak of intolerance for those less intellectual than he.

Once he began writing his list, his wants began to multiply, and soon he had filled over two pages with wants. The central theme of his list was a wish to be accepted by others as he was and to accept himself. He longed for relationships with others and he wanted to like himself. Getting in touch with his wants evidently had an effect on him. In subsequent visits the way he dressed became more relaxed; he slouched in his seat a bit; and he readily smiled and made eye contact.

Some people, especially those who are "not allowed to want," find it difficult to avoid judging themselves as selfish, proud, or simply "bad." One man titled the first page of his list "My Wants," the second page "More Wants," and the third page "More Selfish Wants." He found it very confusing to realize he had so many wants and discovered that by the third page he had delivered a general judgment of selfishness upon himself.

Many people will find themselves resisting writing their wants without judgment, uninhibitedly. Many of us fear to risk total openness—even just to ourselves and to God. Yet that is precisely what this prayer asks us to approach, total openness.

Because we wish to bring our total self to light, including our shadowy and socially unacceptable parts, it is important as we begin prayerfully making a list of wants that we ask God to help us remain clearly focused on this very significant desire: to be more fully alive.

The objectives of this prayer, then, are (1) to make you more fully alive, (2) to be yourself just as you are, (3) to be able to own the hopes and the potentials for growth hidden in your wants, and (4) to be able to see the wishes you may need to let go of.

Writing a wish or a want brings it to the surface of consciousness so its appropriateness may be recognized. Once you clearly see it, you can choose to act on a want or you can let go of it. Sometimes letting go of a destructive wish allows you to become more free, more loving, and more in touch with your capacity to forgive yourself and others. In any case your prayer involves the courage to face the wish, to process its appropriateness, and then to let it go or to go after it.

The List of My Wants Prayer

First, you'll need time to get deeply into the experience, so take an hour all for yourself. Do the activity alone, preferably. If you don't have a private place, go to a library or your car—someplace you are least likely to be disturbed.

Second, take a few minutes to relax and quiet yourself so your wants will flow freely.

Third, express your intention and objectives to God in order to clarify the objectives of your prayer: to release hidden energy and to become more fully alive.

Fourth, you might begin by repeatedly chanting softly the words, "I want, I want, I want." It is important to find some way to hear yourself acknowledge wanting.

Fifth, after chanting for a short while, let your writing of wants begin. Start each line with "I want" and complete the sentence with one of your wants. You may express as many wishes as you like. The more freely you write, the more effective the process. Deeper wishes, usually hidden from consciousness, tend to surface once you are freely and fully into the process. These deeper wants often contain powerful sources of energy that when channeled can help transform your life.

Don't judge or evaluate yourself. Continue writing until it seems there are no more wants inside you. Then stop for a few moments and repeat the chant to see if something else surfaces. Usually there are a few more, sometimes important, wants that just needed an extra push.

When nothing more comes, relax and grow peaceful. Simply let the pages of wants be on the table in front of you or let them rest at your side.

More Ways to Use Your Wants

It is often advisable to save your list of wants until some hours, or even a day, later before you read through them. When you reread them, don't be judgmental. Accept the self that has those wants.

Little by little, one want at a time, begin to sort out the items you really want to actualize in your life. When you come across a want that embarrasses you, ask yourself if you want to keep it or let go of it. Also notice patterns in your list of wants. The young law student's wants fell into two clear categories: those that wished for acceptance from others and those that wished for self-acceptance. Such patterns help clarify where your inner self is ready to direct its energies.

Wants lists can hold keys to breakthroughs out of burnout. For example, in the wants list of a working mother, every single item began with the patterned phrase, "I want more time to" or "I want time to." Here are the first ten items on her list of more than fifty.

I want more time and less pressure.
I want more time to read.
I want more time to write letters.
I want more time to walk.
I want more time to bake.

I want more time to think and reflect.
I want more time to exercise.
I want more time to enjoy nature.
I want time to learn to sing.
I want more time to enjoy my children.

Burned-out people, like this working mother, are apt to feel only one want—for example, not to be interrupted, not to be bothered, not to be hassled, not to be asked, not to be overwhelmed, or not to despair. Note that most of such wants are not active but passive. The working woman began her list with a passive want—"I want more time and less pressure." Although she kept the passive wish for time throughout, she was able in each case to move into more active and concrete wants, thus revealing where certain energies were waiting to be released.

People in burnout should therefore continue writing their lists until they reach a level of active wanting, which will put them in touch with their energy resources and indicate how they could take control of their lives. Wants to be creative, in any domain, usually are active wants.

Wants you choose to live out can become a topic of meditation. (What does this want tell me about myself, my needs, and my energies?) They also can be subject matter for daily decisions. (How can I live more fully by finding ways of acting on my wants?)

Chapter 11

Finding Alternatives

When Ken's wife left him, he became terribly discouraged and lost his identity as a husband. For weeks he walked around after work aimlessly. "There was nothing else to do," he said, as many do who feel they have no alternatives. A friend encouraged him to go to night school. Reluctantly, Ken agreed. Fortunately, the atmosphere at the college he chose turned out to be exciting, and even though Ken had lost his husband identity, he began to discover his student identity. He had found an alternative. Having alternatives is often a source of energy.

The Need for Alternatives

After Rachel's husband died, she was convinced she would become alcoholic. "There was nothing else to do," was her expression, too. But with the help of some friends she discovered there were alternatives to becoming an alcoholic. She moved from the home that was laden with all her sad memories; she changed her eating habits; she began taking vitamins and doing daily exercise; and she took up sewing, which eventually evolved into a successful small business for her.

Being in touch with your alternatives is very helpful in working through times of grief, fear, anxiety, and depression. Finding alternatives is a self-care experience that can take a number of forms, depending on a person's "stuck" place. Some people will need alternatives to help them out of a loss of a relationship, loss of a job, or loss of a home. Others will need alternatives to help them feel better about themselves. Still others will need alternatives upon which to focus their energies during free time, relaxation time, or recovery time.

Burnout people are often bored or frustrated. "I don't know what to do," "There's nothing for me to do," or "I can't think of anything to do." When people feel stuck, useless, or in the way, they clearly need to be acting or thinking differently. They need alternatives.

An important point to remember is that we need alternatives in many areas of life. When Peggy was a little girl, she used to say that God loved her. "I could count on that," she explained, "because I was God's good little girl." But as she grew up, she no longer believed she was a good little girl, so she couldn't believe that God could still love her. Yet she still wanted somebody to love her. Eddy loved her and she became Eddy's girl. Eddy was her alternative. She could turn to him and feel loved and affirmed.

She also discovered that when Eddy wasn't around, she needed others who would affirm her. She joined a group of young people at church, and from them she received feedback about her qualities, which included her caring, sensitivity, intelligence, wit, and also her notable need for frequent reassurance. At times when she lost touch with her own sense of self, she learned to telephone her friends. Eventually, she learned to hear the affirming voice from within herself as well as from outside.

A Trapped Situation

Others need to find places in their lives where they feel a sense of control. There are times when people have no idea whether what they say or do has any effect at all. A social worker wanted to change his profession because he was tired of the bureaucracy, dishonesty, and people trying to beat the system. He tried to be caring yet felt lots of anger at coworkers who seemed simply to be manipulating the system. He felt caught in the middle, frustrated, not knowing what to do with his angry feelings.

Perhaps this social worker's situation is symbolic of all people who feel trapped in a job, a role, a family, a relationship, or a destructive pattern of behaving. Finding alternatives asks you to begin listing alternatives to your trapped situation. For example, when the social worker was asked what kind of work he liked to do, he said, "I like to help people; I want them to feel less frightened in their situation; I like to give them comfort and hope. And I want to make a difference."

Once his objectives were clear, he was asked to list all the occupations he could think of that offered him opportunities to do what he liked to do. He was able to list almost ten other kinds of jobs he could do that satisfied his conditions for a desirable job. After making his list, he thought about each alternative and prayed about it. What happened in the end was that he decided to keep his job as a social worker. Even though the outward situation of his job had not changed, a very important change had happened within him. Knowing he had many alternatives and knowing he could leave his job if necessary, he no longer felt helplessly trapped in his old job.

Exploring his alternatives prayerfully had given him a new perspective about who he was, what he wanted to do in the world, the problems he might encounter in trying to do what he wanted, and other avenues to achieve what he wanted when one pathway didn't work out. In doing this he had gained some modicum of control over his life.

The Finding Alternatives Prayer

The alternatives prayer begins when you realize you are psychologically stuck or trapped or getting stuck is likely to happen to you. The next step is to take your paper and pen and answer questions like the following:

1. What kinds of work (relating, self-concern, self-control, and so on) are most attractive to me? How would I like to express myself in the world?
2. What opportunities are available for me to express myself in the ways I would like to? Make a list of these alternatives.

Afterwards, reflect on your alternatives and be grateful for each one. Resolve to utilize one or another of them if and when necessary.

One woman who often felt overwhelmed and out of control made a list of alternatives that she discovered would help calm her down. "Just knowing that I have my list is sometimes enough to get me settled," she said.

People feel frustrated and helpless in facing the problem of losing weight. How they look and feel in their body is important to them. Is there anything to do for those who have tried "all the diets"? Try the alternatives prayer.

Dealing with Fears

One child in therapy was locked into fear of losing something, and finding alternatives offered him a way out. His fear was that while he and his family were living in New York (his father, a professor, was on a one-year sabbatical exchange) the exchange family living in their California home would burn it down; he would lose his home and have nothing to return to at the end of the year. "And if they burn my house down, I'll kill them," he asserted.

The therapist asked if he had any alternatives other than killing the people, since killing them wouldn't bring his house back. "Then I'll make them build my house again, exactly as it was." He was insistent that the house be exactly as he left it.

The therapist asked that since they would have to build the house completely again, wouldn't he like to have some change made, perhaps in his own room. He thought for a minute and then said, "I'd like my window to be a picture window." And after another pause, he added, "I'd like it to have a window seat." A few minutes later he got in touch with a wish to move the location of his California home to a lake. From there on, filled with alternatives, he went on to completely designing his own home. He was no longer frightened at the possibility of losing something. Rather, the alternatives he thought of expressed many opportunities for some new and wonderful things to come into his life.

Having alternatives helps overcome many kinds of fears. One woman told her story:

> Whenever I have to run a party, especially after a hard day at work, I tend to get frantic wanting to make sure everything is done perfectly and that everyone has a good time. I never enjoyed getting frantic. Then I discovered that I didn't have to accept responsibility for other people having a good time. So I am learning to look forward to my parties as a way of *my* enjoying a good time with my friends. I still do all the work, but I am letting go of worrying about things over which I have no control.

She realized also that it was the responsibility of her guests to enjoy each other. Her own new relaxedness allowed those enjoyable interactions among her guests to happen naturally.

Assuming responsibility that isn't yours can burn you out quickly. A personal counselor at a small college said, "Whenever I feel it's my responsibility to care for *all* the emotional needs and problems at the college, I'm taking on an impossible task and it's easy to slip into burnout, especially when I begin to believe that I have no alternatives."

Having alternatives gives a sense of having some control over your life and what happens to you. Having alternatives is a source of strength and a way of caring for yourself when you may be burning yourself out.

Chapter 12

Handicaps

Each of us is handicapped in some way. Some of us have obvious physical defects that come from genetic inheritance or the effects of disease; and for most of us our bodies don't work perfectly. Something or other in the bones, muscles, nerves, blood, or organs gives us trouble. Many people have mental or emotional handicaps; these include learning disabilities, a tendency to anxiety or depression, neuroses, phobias, compulsions, a NOT-OK personality, an inability to relate intimately, and an out-of-touchness with feelings. Many people also have spiritual handicaps, such as an inability to make decisions and carry them out, a lack of courage, a lack of self-affirmation, the inability to forgive or to create or to discern truth, or a lack of meaning and purpose in their lives.

It is very valuable to be in touch with your handicaps, to realize where in you are the physical, psychological, and spiritual wounds, for wounds are the vulnerable points in your system. Wounds often use up energy; wounded places in people usually have less stamina; wounds can cause you to be drained. And people often experience burnout in relation to their handicaps and wounds.

Some Common Handicaps

A woman described her handicap as feeling she must take on the weight of the whole world. "I feel that I must carry everything, that I must be responsible for whatever happens to anyone around me, that this burden is on my shoulders." She feels she must be totally available at her job, available to her in-laws, available at the church, available to her children, available to her husband, available for the PTA, available to her mother, available to her sister, and available to her neighbors. This sense of responsibility for everything is really a handicap and can easily lead to burnout, for she seriously undervalues her own life, health, and enjoyment and cannot see the need for being responsible for herself.

Another likely candidate for burnout is the person handicapped by the need to be needed, wishing to be the most important person in a family or group by being needed by everyone. Such people tend to see other people as more handicapped than themselves and tend to want to keep other people handicapped, like the wife who realized she had lost her important role of being needed by her alcoholic husband when he joined Alcoholics Anonymous. Needing to be needed can be a very healthy human wish when the needing is reasonable; once the needing becomes excessive, it becomes a handicap. Needing to be needed as a personality wound can afflict people of any age.

Another closely related handicap among busy people is the conviction that, "I should be able to do it all by myself." Healing here happens when I can let someone help me, when I can share the burden, when I can let myself feel the interdependence of human living.

Getting in Touch with Your Handicaps

What does it feel like to be wounded? How do people get in touch with their handicaps? Look first at some of the psychological scars you may be carrying: scars of failures in school, scars of being fired from a job or rejected in a relationship, scars of putdowns and refusals from significant people, scars of severe discipline during childhood, scars of being embarrassed or laughed at during younger years, scars from misguided training or disturbing experiences in sexuality, scars from any painful, frightening, or confusing experiences.

Look next at the people and the situations you tend to avoid or run away from. What are the things you are scared of? Where are the tender spots in your personality, the ones that seem always to be getting bumped? What are the situations in which your feelings can get hurt? Who are the people who can make you feel NOT-OK? How do they have this effect on you? These are some places to look for your woundedness.

Some common forms of woundedness or handicaps include perfectionism, carelessness, workaholism, blaming or projecting responsibility onto others, a sense of inferiority, consumerism, prejudices, various addictions, inability to rest or enjoy oneself, being out of touch with one's feelings, predisposition to failure, chronic complaining, and sexual obsessions. All these areas, and many more, are suitable themes for the handicap prayer.

The Handicap Prayer

To do the handicap prayer, the first step is to become conscious of one of your handicaps and own that it is yours at this time. Own your vulnerability.

Next, ask the spirit that lives deep within you how you originally acquired this wound and how it relates to the ways you deal with pressures and burnout in your life. Spend some time quietly observing the answers and insights that occur to you.

Finally, ask God if there isn't something you can do about this handicap. If you can't overcome it, perhaps you can transform your view of it.

The Strength in Weakness

Wounds usually leave effects on us that last a very long time. The dancer who strained his back at age seventeen will probably have for the rest of his life a slight weak spot where that strain occurred. The woman whose ego was shattered by a childhood trauma will, till the day she dies, be especially vulnerable to similar attacks. People who are peculiarly susceptible to envy, jealousy, a violent temper, lust, or some other excessive distortion of spiritual energies can probably count on having that susceptibility for a very long time. The reformed alcoholic is still an alcoholic and will be for every single day of his or her life, a fact that Alcoholics Anonymous recognizes.

The first point in all this is that if you have a handicap or a pathology, you can count on it being a more or less permanent dimension of your life. Therefore you can also count on it being integrated into your life's journey and into your call from God. A wise psychologist spoke of one's pathology as one's path. Any true call from God will be a call that integrates not only your abilities and gifts but also your handicaps. Like Jesus, you will carry your wounds with you to heaven.

The second point about handicaps is that God's love seems to be intensified and increased toward people who are physically, psychologically, or socially handicapped or wounded. Therefore persons who own their handicaps as part of the kingdom can count on being specially blessed by God. Jesus' Sermon on the Mount assures us that God blesses the poor, the hungry, the widows, those treated unjustly, the rejected, and many others we would never suspect to be God's favorites. So in our handicap prayer we can remind God of the special love promised us by Jesus.

The third point is that where we are handicapped, we can call upon the Christ to make up for what is lacking in us. So if we lack courage ourselves, we can proceed to act courageously, confident that the grace and courage of the Christ will act through us, supplying whatever is lacking in us. The Apostle Paul was glad for his woundedness because each of his wounded places was one where the Christ spirit had filled him. It was as if the more he was wounded, the more he would be filled with the Christ life (see 2 Cor. 12:7–10).

How Handicaps Affect Others

Handicaps in people also have their effects on others. Your handicap is an opportunity for someone else's gifts to be used, thereby bringing the two of you together. Reciprocally, someone else's handicap is an opportunity for you to use your gifts, again with the result that you and they are connected in caring ways.

An older couple had a retarded child. Instead of institutionalizing her, they kept her at home and struggled, using their own gifts of love and patience to bring her up as normally as they could. Though she would never be able to live in the world alone, they creatively discovered ways to socialize their daughter, even to the point of her being able to read and to help with the cooking. Instead of being a burden, they viewed her as a gift and counted the riches of their life with her. The benefits to the parents were many. First of all, they enjoyed the special privilege of having a child at home longer than parents of normal children. Second, they watched with awe and wonder the marvelous pattern of human growth as it played itself out in their daughter. Most parents have children who grow so fast they cannot even observe the process; these parents were able to watch the growth process in slow motion. Third, the techniques the parents developed in socializing their retarded daughter were so creative they were asked to do a film on them and to give seminars to share what they had learned from their experience. Fourth, and most important, they were blessed with a happy child.

Seeing handicapped people can touch off deep caring places in our hearts. It can trigger in us a desire to help others to become whole persons, a desire to become whole persons ourselves, a desire to make the world a more whole place to live in. Interacting with a few handicapped people started Jean Vanier on a lifetime career of establishing L'Arche communities for handicapped people all over the world. Dorothy Day was so moved by the plight of the poor working person that she founded the Catholic Worker Mission on the Lower East Side of New York. Today there are many Catholic Worker houses across the nation. Experiencing victims of racial and sexual discrimination has inspired people to become involved in racial justice and equal rights organizations, thereby bringing a bit more wholeness into individual lives and into society.

Caring among members of a family is often sparked by a physical or psychological wound experienced by one member. Wounding sometimes allows caring to take place.

Chapter 13

Letter Writing

A therapist said that her patients sometimes write letters to her. In such letters, after the writers have expressed their feelings, they seem to reach a place where they articulate their problems and almost seem to hear a reply coming, not from her but from within themselves, and they know what they need to do. For this reason they usually do not even share their letters with the therapist, for her role, as a bridge to their own inner wisdom, is already being fulfilled. In addressing themselves to her now, they utilize her as a focusing agent, channel, or bridge to levels of knowledge they may not realize they possess.

She told of a series of actual letters written by a college student she had seen as a high school senior. Before the therapist had gotten around to answering the student's first letter from college, which voiced almost overwhelming feelings about her family relationships, a second letter arrived saying that just writing the first letter had brought things into perspective. Writing it had tuned her into the therapist's way of reflecting, and she had discovered what she had to do to deal with her problem. A third letter from the student indicated she had put her new self-knowledge into action and was progressing well.

Writing tends to spiritualize both deep sadness and bubbly joy. It adds a dimension that transforms a powerfully lived experience into something connected to God. In writing we get insights into details and meanings of life that somehow come out on paper in clarifying statements. This is an experience of grace, for such letter writing puts you in touch with your own spirit and your need to value yourself, which is the area of God's action. In other words, the very act of writing is an experience of God at work in you.

The Letter Writing Prayer

The first step, before you actually begin writing words on paper, is to visualize the person or object you're addressing. Imagine them standing nearby so you can release the full force of your feelings. The previously mentioned student said she used to picture herself talking to the therapist in face-to-face conversation.

The second step is to ask God's spirit to make your letter writing a healing experience, to clarify the roots of your pressure, hurt, or burnout, and to have the courage to act on the gifts of insight that come to you through the letter writing.

Third, take out a piece of paper or a tablet and begin writing about who you are and how you're feeling. For example, if your boss has been criticizing your work and saying you are not living up to his or her expectations, compose a letter to your boss explaining your view of what has been happening at work. Mention who you are in your deepest self and how he or she probably does not see the parts of you that go beyond the work situation but that you want to affirm that these parts are there inside you and are very valuable. Write about the parts of you and your life that are good and valuable but unappreciated in the present situation.

Even when writing in the context of prayer, it is important to let your anger and frustrations out as you write, if that is what is inside wanting to come out. No need to hide your feelings from God for God is more aware of them than you are. Be honest about your feelings. If you feel hurt or abused, let your pen express what you feel. God wants to relate to the totality that is you, not just to your "nice person" mask, for example. God is someone you don't have to cover up with.

Use any pressure situation or relationship—at home, at school, on the job, or in the neighborhood—as subject matter for a letter prayer.

Letter prayers may be addressed to the people or events that have provoked a strong pressure-making response in you, or you may address them to God, holy figures, friends, historic characters, entities from your dreams, teachers, imaginary persons, or even to some deep part of yourself—anyone who could evoke your capacity to share yourself fully. God is active in your life through all such channels.

The fourth step of the letter writing prayer, when the letter is written, is to thank God for the experience and for the privilege to have gotten in touch with deep energy sources within you.

A Letter of Introduction

A young woman found that letter writing helped her in a time of grief. At her father's funeral, each of the immediate family was asked to put something special in the coffin. Her mother put in a rosary and one of her brothers put in a fish lure to honor the special moments of closeness they had experienced going fishing together. The young woman put in a letter she had written, a letter of introduction to heaven telling everyone there who her father was, his specialness, his personal likes and dislikes, what she would most miss from him, and asking God to make a place for him there.

The letter writing fostered many healthy psychological and spiritual processes in her, especially a sense of closure in saying goodbye to the physical presence of her father. Her letter, hoping to help facilitate a transition for her father, mirrored her own need to adjust; her own identity had begun a transition and needed to be redefined. With the death of her father she had moved into the next generation to face death, and she needed to grow into a comfortable inner place with that knowledge and to come to terms with her understanding of death and after death in a more intimate way.

Letter prayers like this young woman's involve the whole person. The body does the writing; the feelings and the thoughts of the mind are expressing themselves; and the spirit is opening itself to the grace of self-awareness and self-valuing.

Some Variations

If the person you visualize as you write begins to respond within you, you may write dialogue instead of a simple letter. While a letter often expresses only one side of an issue, dialogue gives a person involved in your situation a chance to speak. Thus as you write, each "I say" is followed by a "You say."

Another variation is to write poetry. This doesn't mean you need to make lines of your letter rhyme but rather you may use individual words or phrases instead of sentences and you can begin expressing each new idea or image on a new line. You may also place words and phrases in different positions on the page. One woman in her letters often stacks words above and below the line to express other dimensions

pains

wishes   insights

of her feelings and thoughts

sensitivities   concerns

frustrations

You may want to insert sketches or draw symbols on the page. Use whatever helps express what is happening inside you.

Another important point about actually writing something on paper is that you can hold the writing in your hand; you can read it aloud, share it with someone, or save it to read again at another time.

Letter Writing at Important Times

Letter prayers need not always be a response to anger, sadness, or frustration. They are helpful, too, in times of joy and meaningfulness. For example, you may write letter prayers at important times: when you get a new job, when you graduate, when you discover you're pregnant, or when you meet someone special for the first time. All of these are important passages in your life. When you write letter prayers at these times, try to say what you're feeling and how you got to this place in your life. Spell out your expectations, hopes, wishes, and wants in all the ways and words you can. Conclude the letter with a renewed dedication of yourself to doing God's will. All prayer letters may be saved and reread when you want to look back and review the stepping-stones of your life.

Automatic Writing

A special form of writing a letter prayerfully, called automatic writing, provides a special way of access to levels of inner wisdom, to the voice of the soul and the voice of God within.

To focus clearly on God's presence as you do automatic writing, begin with a few moments of quiet, making a request that you be spoken to by God, that you will hear something you need to hear. Then start writing—words, phrases, whatever—with the expectation that you will hear what you need to hear. Don't try to form words and sentences; simply let your hand write. Let go of any control. Write whatever appears in your head. You can always go back afterward and fill in the missing words. The important thing is to let it flow freely. Continue writing until you have a sense that the message has come to an end.

The writing may not look at all like your usual writing. In fact, you may experience the automatic writing as someone other than yourself writing to you.

A few months ago a woman was in a period of confusion and anxiety, looking for reassurance. She wanted to know what was going on in her life. She needed to know she was on the right path, she was doing God's will, because all sorts of experiences were happening inside and outside her that she couldn't make sense of. In automatic writing she consciously directed her writing to her "inner me," feeling a need to dialogue with this deep core self, to make peace with it, to reassure it of her love.

By the second paragraph her inner me began to reply, pouring out words of wisdom and reassuring her that her life was moving in a good direction. Near the end of the letter this inner guide told her she could get in touch with it whenever she really needed to do so. She was cautioned, however, that she should not use this process thoughtlessly or habitually for insignificant problems, in which cases she was encouraged to find answers using her own experience and wits. She was to value and make use of the part of her that had learned to operate in the outer world.

In letter writing or other activities that delve deeply into the inner world and its symbols and our inner and outer selves, it is important to keep inner and outer wisdom in balance in their complementary contribution to the totality of our lives.

Part IV

Prayerways: Physical Activity

Chapter 14

Habitual Activities

If you can't take time out from your normal activities to pray or if the time you take out for prayer turns out to be a frustrating experience, then try turning your habitual activities into a prayer. Simply take some pleasant experience you are planning to do and as you begin it, offer it to God as your prayer. Next, proceed with your activity as usual: combing your hair, brushing your teeth, making beds, sorting mail, reading a newspaper, driving to work, cooking meals, walking the dog, putting children to bed, sweeping the floor, and so on.

If you like, you can add another prayerful dimension—a symbolic transformation—to your habitual activities. Each evening during her performance of *South Pacific* Mary Martin shampooed her hair; but while she did it, she symbolically transformed her activity by singing the words, "I'm gonna wash that man right out of my hair."

In a similar way, your habitual activities may be symbolically transformed. For example, we asked three people what taking a shower might mean to them on a symbolic level. The first said she would take a shower to wash away all her tensions, worries, the residue of her negative feelings, the effects of the day's harassments, her tiredness, and "those little particles of worries that you can't do anything about."

The second said he would make his shower a meditation of

forgiveness, looking forward to coming away cleansed, to be self-forgiven and God-forgiven, to be renewed and sparkling and "free of the greyness of life."

The third said that during showering she would be grateful for each part of her body. As she washed her feet she would thank them for all the waiting and standing they do; she would thank her knees for all the stooping and bending they do and so on all the way to the top of her head.

Seeing Habitual Activities Symbolically

Driving to work, a daily activity for many people, may symbolically be viewed as one's way of moving forward in the world, the car itself revealing one's emotional and spiritual energy systems.

Many habitual activities involve eating and food. Eating meals may symbolize a nourishment of the whole self, a caring for oneself. The digestion and elimination processes may symbolize the cycle of taking in and integrating the good and letting go of what is unusable and unhelpful.

Emptying the garbage may symbolize getting rid of things we no longer need and would be unhealthy to keep inside any longer. Cooking symbolizes preparing energies to be consumed and used. Chewing your food may symbolize the parts of you that continue to work and process, even though you're worn out, and the parts of you that continue to serve even when forgotten. These nourishment symbols may be especially helpful for people in time of burnout.

Transforming the Act of Waiting

Waiting, at grocery stores, in doctors' offices, at red lights, or wherever, may also be transformed into prayer by allowing the waiting moments to become moments for relaxing, for creating a peaceful space. Instead of building up frustration at waiting, instead even of using artifical and possibly unwelcome stimulation to pass the time (such as listening to a radio, flipping through a magazine, or overlistening to conversation), create your own environment with your imagination. Instead of being an energy drain, the moments of waiting can invite an increase of inner energy.

A Focus on Hands

One busy mother said she often does the habitual activities prayer by focusing on her hands. She offers to God all that her hands do during the day: cooking, washing, feeding, writing letters, brushing a child's hair, rubbing someone's back, touching someone in love, or slapping someone in anger. She also becomes conscious of the many hands that touch her and her life.

Psychologically, the way hands are drawn by a person can represent how one sees oneself getting one's needs met. Spiritually, hands represent the mode of one's giving and receiving spiritual energies. Blessings are most often bestowed with a gesture of the hands. Just before the most solemn moments of the Catholic mass, priests wash their hands, asking to be cleansed of their iniquity so they are clean to touch and distribute holy communion as a blessing.

Whatever habitual activities you choose to focus upon, you may present the doing of them to God as a prayer, an offering that symbolizes you or some part of you wishing to honor God or express your love to God.

Chapter 15

Doing What You Like

If you're slipping down into burnout or into too much pressure, don't wait until you collapse or until the doctor orders you into the hospital for a rest. Stop your downward spiral, your burnout cycle. Turn yourself around. You will be better able to do all the work you have to do if you are alive and energized than if you are totally exhausted.

If it seems too much for you to declare a week or even a whole day off for yourself, then start small. But please begin. When burned out, people can serve neither God nor their fellow humans.

For you it will surely be a prayer to give your system a chance to rest and reenergize itself. For you treating yourself to some things you like to do would certainly be a way of saying thanks to God for the gift of your life and for the gift of being aware of your needs.

The Prayer Format

Begin this prayer by making a list of small things you like to do. Some of the things that might occur to you include having breakfast in bed, asking grandma to take care of the children for the weekend, shutting off the telephone for the entire evening, window shopping for an afternoon, picnicking in the park, spending a quiet evening with a loving friend, taking a bubble bath, looking through photo albums or yearbooks, walking along the ocean, looking out the window and day-dreaming, listening to records, dancing, writing poetry or making an entry in your personal journal, trying on the clothes in the closet that haven't been worn in years, or rereading old letters.

The second step is to set aside time, every day if possible, to do one or more of the things on your list. A counselor tells his way of finding time to do what he likes: "Everyone begins work at our offices at nine o'clock. I decided to begin my day half an hour early, before other people arrived. I use the half hour strictly as my own spiritual time, sitting, meditating, reading, even napping. As long as I keep my door closed, people don't bother me since they presume I am seeing a client. They're correct. The client is me."

The third step is to offer each activity to God as a gift of love to yourself and to God.

One very busy clergyman responded to this prayer with an explanation that went something like this: "God loves me and asks me to love myself. In his love for me God puts all the things on my list in the world as possibilities. In my cooperation with God's love for me I take the next step and turn these possibilities into reality. So when I do one of the things I like to do, I'm sort of giving myself a gift from God."

Something Extraordinary

In order to have the effect of breaking your burnout cycle and turning you around, it helps if you do something that you wouldn't ordinarily do.

A young married woman told how her father-in-law would give her money for Christmas, telling her to use the money in treating herself to something she ordinarily wouldn't treat herself to. His delight was in giving her that possibility. And when she treated herself, she would share with him how she had used his gift. Once she found a scarlet velvet coat on sale, marked way down. So she bought it, then took it to show her father-in-law. They both delighted in how it looked on her and in the bargain it was.

This woman's story might be used symbolically as a model for the do something you like prayer. First, she turned to the father and accepted the gift; it was a gift she could use in many different ways. Second, she used the gift to do something she delighted in, knowing it was all happening in an atmosphere of love. Third, she returned and shared her joy with the father.

A Chance to Be Creative

It is important to remember to be resourceful and creative in adding little delights to your life. For many people in burnout everything feels the same, day in and day out; everything turns into a dull and burdensome drag. To counter this—the intent of this prayer—begin with something simple yet let it be something you wouldn't ordinarily do, like moving a piece of furniture in your house or treating yourself to a small plant or flower and putting it where you will see it most.

Allowing that many people in the burnout cycle are on diets for overweight, heart conditions, blood pressure, or ulcers, there are some whose list of things might contain treats like a hot fudge sundae or lemon meringue pie. If these items are on your forbidden list, find something else, maybe not food, that would delight you. Then allow yourself, as a prayer of caring for yourself, to surfeit yourself in some delicious experience.

By the way, this is not a prayer to encourage consumerism. The most effective forms of this prayer are very inexpensive ones. As the old song says, "The best things in life are free." Here might be included spending time in the mountains or watching birds in the backyard or sunlight playing on the leaves.

A man who had insomnia told how he learned to transform his thinking about his insomnia. "On insomnia nights, instead of worrying about not getting enough sleep, I would get out of bed and use the time as a gift to myself—maybe read a book or treat myself to a late show. Often I found I fell asleep on the couch. It was as restful as sleeping—or not sleeping—in my bed."

A mother of three young children at first found it hard to get any free time for herself. Like the counselor mentioned earlier, she decided to wake up an hour before everyone else and gift herself with that hour. Usually, she made a cup of coffee and just sat alone in the living room, treating the time as a kind of meditation period. A mother with a busy schedule and a large family said, "The only time I have privacy is when I'm in the shower." She took many relaxing, time-to-herself showers.

Maintaining a Sense of Giftedness

One caution is in order here. Since the intent of this prayer mode is to break a burnout cycle and to keep the sense of something different—a gift—alive, it's important that you look forward to your treat each day or each week. One man who decided to take a course in a continuing education program found himself after the third class saying, "Well I signed up for this darn course, now I'll have to keep going to it every week." Such an attitude is not helpful, especially for a person under stress. For him the class had become simply one more obligation, one more burden, one more pressure point in an already stress-filled schedule. It would be better, in his case, to stop going to the class and plan to use the time in another way, where he could keep the giftedness of the time as the primary value.

Music as Gift

Ideas for unusual treats sometimes come from others. A young man visited a friend who had stereo speakers in his bathroom, so he decided he would hook up in his bathroom the extra pair of speakers he had put away in his closet. He found it a treat to have music while he was in the bathroom, especially in the morning. "It's the nicest thing I've done for myself in a long time," he said.

Music is a special gift of God, full of healing powers. Let its energy fill your life. If your budget doesn't allow you to buy new records, you can usually buy them for a fraction of their original cost at garage sales or borrow them from the public library.

God gifts us with so many possibilities. One of our responses can be to make some of these possibilities real. Pass this prayer on. Tell others of it. It's a kind of prayer you don't mind telling people about.

Chapter 16

Doing Something Else

Finding alternatives (Chapter 11) focused on people who feel fearful and stuck in their jobs, in permanent relationships, or in other serious situations. This chapter focuses on less serious situations but those that nonetheless by their frequency or predictability continue to debilitate and wear down even valiant spirits.

The Pressure of Waiting

Waiting is probably the commonest such situation. Waiting is a continually predictable part of life: waiting for buses, planes, trains; waiting in dentists' offices, doctors' offices, hospitals, or at business appointments; waiting in supermarket lines, at stop lights, in traffic jams, in banks, in department stores and shops; waiting for guests to arrive; waiting for the phone to ring; and waiting for test results. On and on goes the list. Life today moves at a hectic pace. Everybody is hurrying. "Hurry up and wait" sums up contemporary life for many people.

And what do people do while waiting? What do they think of? Most people's minds are not into the waiting. They may be complaining about having to wait. They may be worried about being late for some other event, or they simply "waste time."

In any case, whether people respond to waiting by seething, being bored, blaming others, or having a cigarette, these responses don't usually nurture human growth.

For example, if you are sitting waiting for a plane and would prefer not to waste your time, you can do something else. Try writing a letter, relive a nice memory, do some reflection and meditation, say a prayer for someone, talk to someone nearby, perhaps to another person alone, explore your openness to new people and things, or fantasize what you'd most like to be doing at this moment. Although in forced waiting time you may not have much control over your external life, you still have the choice of control over your internal life.

While waiting is often boring or frustrating, waiting can also be frightening, as was the case with this young woman:

> I was waiting for my young daughter's operation in the hospital. I couldn't tolerate being inside the hospital, so I came outside and walked. I found myself using each sidewalk square as a prayer place. As I walked, I stopped and focused at the center of each square and said a prayer. One one block I'd say, "Please, God, make the operation be successful." On the next, "Let her know I love her." And on the next, "Let her get well soon." And so on.

For this woman waiting was transformed. Each step became an opportunity to create her own prayer. Stopping and focusing on each square of sidewalk took the focus off her anxiety and placed her energy in the ritual movement and in getting in touch with her deepest wishes. While anxiety consumes energy, praying and centering generated energy for her.

Feeling Disorganized and Uncreative

Besides waiting, there are other situations where "doing something else" might be appropriate and helpful, for example, when you can't seem to get organized, when you can't seem to get centered, when your creativity isn't flowing well, when you are bored with your usual daily routine, when you need a change in your life, or when you are in a blocked or obsessive situation (that is, when you can't seem to do something correctly and yet you keep on trying and each try fails worse than the last).

Robin had to make a presentation to a group of graduate students, but, hard as she tried, she couldn't get her thoughts organized. Her roommate suggested she simply do something else. "When this once happened to me," the roommate explained, "I cleaned my closet." So Robin decided to try cleaning her room, and as she let go of her worry and began arranging her desk drawers and her room, the presentation began to organize itself in her mind. An hour later, effortlessly, it had clarified itself, and Robin gave a fine presentation to her group.

A young mother who faces a daily barrage of yelling and screaming from her six youngsters decided to stop for half an hour every day to darn socks. Surprisingly, not only did the darning calm her down, but it had a quieting effect on the children, too. It also became a time when she would invite one or another of them to sit with her. "Two of the girls even wanted to learn to darn socks," she said.

Unfriendly Situations

When you are faced with what seems like an unfriendly situation (for example, at a meeting or a party with strangers) and you can't leave, instead of wallowing in fear or discomfort, ask yourself how you can make the meeting an inviting place to spend time. For example, fantasize what each person present does in his or her private life and what you would like to say to each one. You might actually approach one person and introduce yourself and share your fantasy.

Making a Something Else List

It is often helpful to have a list of "something elses," since when people are in a low, tired, or anxious state of mind, they are usually not very spontaneously creative in thinking of things to do that would refresh and energize them. Here's where a variety of lists may be helpful.

One list might contain *things you've always wanted to do*: taking a free class in watercolor painting, studying yoga, singing in a choir, joining a group that reads plays or discusses books, finding a place—maybe a volunteer organization—where you could make some new friends, visiting secondhand stores, or taking a part-time job, especially if it's something you've always wanted to do.

Another list might contain *things that absorb your mind*: playing cards, doing a puzzle, painting, practicing a musical instrument, planting flowers, cleaning desk drawers, sorting files, sorting children's clothes, shopping, doing mechanical things, working in the tool shop, repairing things, looking at catalogues, watching television, going to plays or movies, sewing, writing letters, baking, telephoning friends, keeping a diary, buying a new hat, writing a poem, or playing tennis.

Another list that active people find energizing is one that contains all the little *things around the house that need to be done and that when done provide a sense of accomplishment.*

Make your own lists of things to do. Keep them handy; get used to using them as supports. In times of burnout these lists may provide you with activities that don't take a lot of energy to do and give you a sense of getting things done.

At its deepest level doing something else prayerfully is an act of surrender to God. It says, "I can't seem to do what I'm supposed to, so I'll leave it in your hands and begin doing something else."

The Prayer Format

The doing something else prayer may be summarized in the following three steps:

1. Acknowledge you are in a stuck place where your wheels keep spinning but you can't get out of the rut. Acknowl-

edge your boredom, frustration, or fear and your inability to control it.

2. Surrender the outcome of the situation to God, acknowledging your concern for the situation but also your finiteness to do anything more about it.

3. Consult one of your lists, if necessary, and begin doing something else (that doesn't take too much energy and gives you a sense of satisfaction or enjoyment) and offer it to God as a prayer of trust that God will take care of the original situation.

Chapter 17

Dancing

A nurse at a large university hospital learned to work out her psychological frustrations by dancing them out. After a particularly stressful day, she comes back to her room, plays some music that invites vigorous dancing, and lets her body begin expressing its frustrations in movements in time to the music. "It's really liberating," she commented. "I get out all my frustrations, work up a sweat, and hop into the shower. I'm really grateful for the gift of dancing."

In such personalized dancing you invite your body to act out in movement its psychological and spiritual feelings—of joy, exaltation, sorrow, confusion, acceptance, anger, fear, supplication, and so on. Practically any variety of experience or emotion can be dramatized through movement.

Dancing also has a long history of being related to religious ritual and spiritual energy. Although religious dancing is primarily carried out in churches, there is no reason it cannot be done in one's own personal space. For people under stress the dancing prayer takes a simple five-step format.

The Dancing Prayer Format

First, become conscious of the feelings or emotions that are strongest in you at the moment. Perhaps you feel lonely because a friend has gone away, you are angry at something a friend did to you, or you feel you are getting overextended at home or on the job. Whatever it is, become aware of its presence and power in you now.

Second, find some appropriate music or sound that would help you release your strong feelings and perhaps some object on which to focus your dancing. One college woman, angry at her boyfriend, placed his picture in the middle of the floor and did a warpath dance around it. Another student, lonely for her boyfriend, held his photo in her hands and danced as if he were dancing with her.

Third, present your dancing to God as a prayer for healing and growth. Ask that your pressures be relieved and new strengths begin to flow into you. Be as specific as you can about the pressures and about asking for the energies you need.

Fourth, do your dance, allowing yourself to let go of any self-consciousness about what you're doing. Improvise your movements. Use your hands, head, and hips. Add appropriate facial gestures and make whatever sounds you feel like making. At times you will find you are spontaneously creating a ritual. Don't be surprised. Humans are by nature ritual makers.

Fifth, when you are tired or when your feeling seems to have integrated or departed, you may bring your dancing to a close. At this point say a word of thanks to God for the opportunity of this experience.

Dancing in Your Imagination

When the dancing prayer is done alone, it may be expressed in physical movements as described or it may be done completely in the active imagination. The imagination is used when physical movements are impossible or inappropriate. In this case the dancing prayer follows the same five steps, except that the dancing is carried on in the mind rather than in the body. The imaginative approach has the advantage of allowing the dancer to dance with consummate skill, to perform physical feats that transcend the body's capacities, to bring other people into the scene, and to have the experience in any place the mind can visualize.

Dancing with a Partner

The dancing prayer may also be done with a partner or partners. In this case you may inform your partner, if you wish, that for you this dancing is a prayer and that through it you are offering your feelings of, say, anger or gratitude to God.

While dancing with a partner may be used to release strong negative emotions, it tends to be most appropriate for expressing feelings of union, togetherness, and flowing. When unitive feelings are prominent, become aware of the subtleties and sensitivities of your partner and of his or her movements; notice, too, how the partner's movement affects your own; see how your movements are felt and reacted to by your partner; and feel the coordination and cooperation that the two bodies experience in an atmosphere of music. Their movement as a single unit helps one realize there are places where the loneliness can be broken.

Dancing with a partner also symbolizes the process of understanding that needs to happen psychologically and spiritually between people who wish to interact in loving, caring ways. When two people consciously do the dancing prayer together, one or both of them may formulate gratitude to God for the experience.

Chapter 18

Wrestling

People wrestle a lot, whether they do it physically, in their mind, in their dreams, or spiritually. Jacob wrestled all night with God's messenger (Gen. 32:24). Ben Sirach in the Book of Ecclesiasticus speaks of his soul wrestling to possess wisdom (51:25). Paul the Apostle, talking about a spiritual war, says, "our wrestling is not against flesh and blood, but against . . . the spiritual hosts of wickedness in the heavenly places" (Eph. 6:12).

Wrestling, then, is an activity we are called to whenever we are involved in a struggle—within ourselves, as wrestling with a problem or struggling with a decision or in confronting another person or spirit, as Jacob did. Such struggles and confrontations call for a show of strength.

Wrestling's purpose, when done in a context of prayer, is not to see who is stronger or who wins, as in a professional wrestling match, but more precisely, to reveal where your strengths lie, where your opponent's (partner's) strengths lie, and in what areas you or your opponent (partner) is stronger. Wrestling is one of the few experiences where these qualities may be tested and where energies may be experienced with clear awareness.

People under severe stress or near burnout have been wrestling for a long time with something or someone, whether they know it or not. To bring this combat into consciousness is the objective of wrestling in prayer.

Wrestling in Your Imagination

One way of wrestling prayerfully is to use your creative imagination to carry on a wrestling match between you and your opponent, for example, the source of your burnout or stress.

Workshop participants, accompanied by music from Stravinsky's *Rite of Spring*, imaginatively relive Jacob's all-night wrestling match with God's messenger. Many participants get involved in the struggle and some even identify with Jacob. After seven or eight minutes, participants, who have merely been lying comfortably on the floor, report being tired, strained, exhausted, and sometimes exhilarated—depending on their styles of struggle. For example, some people want to stop the fight between Jacob and the messenger; their whole attitude toward conflict is to stop it when it happens and to avoid it whenever possible. Others really plunge into the wrestling, enjoying the display of energy, thriving on the contest; feeling the conflict itself releases unsuspected energies in them. Others want to run away from the conflict. Still others feel guilty about wrestling, though they continue the combat with intensity. Others turn the wrestling into a kind of ritualistic dance, where nobody is meant to win except according to the script. The point is that the way you wrestle in your imagination can reveal to you, symbolically, how you tend to deal with problems (by avoidance, giving up, running away, feeling guilty, jumping in, dancing back and forth, and so on).

Thus when you wrestle in your imagination, watch your style of dealing with your conflict as it is revealed in the inner drama. See how your inner images speak to you of your way of dealing with your own discouragement, anger, burnout, and anxiety. Perhaps it will tell you your current (and probably in-

effective) way of fighting. Perhaps it will suggest more whole-
some alternatives.

The Wrestling Prayer

Done in the imaginative style, the wrestling prayer format
has five steps:

1. Personify the partner or opponent with whom you are in
   conflict. Give it a face and bodily features so you and it
   would be able physically, though in imagination, to wrestle with each other.
2. Petition God for the gift of insight into your unhelpful
   styles of dealing with conflict and to see alternative ways
   of responding to it.
3. Use your imagination, with appropriate combative music
   playing in the background, to initiate a wrestling match.
   Carry on the wrestling in your imagination for as long as
   you need to. You will know when a stopping place occurs.
   By the way, as you fantasize the wrestling, let your hands
   and legs and whole body express themselves. Spontaneous physical movements usually help intensify imaginative experience.
4. When the fantasy is complete, thank God for the experience and for any awarenesses that have come to you.
5. Review your fantasy, clarifying and evaluating the effectiveness of your response style to conflict manifested in
   the fantasy.

Physical Wrestling

There is another way to wrestle prayerfully, which is a very
powerful and self-revealing process. It is to wrestle physically
with a closely trusted partner. The combatants could be close
friends, of the same or opposite sex, marriage partners, or siblings. Usually there is between friends, lovers, partners, and

siblings, despite protestations of closeness, oneness, and harmony, underlying conflicts as yet unspoken and consequently
unresolved. Energy is unconsciously expended in keeping
these conflicts beneath the surface. People wrestle verbally, often with extreme subtlety, and conflictual matters seldom seem
to get resolved. Without bringing these hidden conflicts fully
to consciousness, physical wrestling can help relieve the tensions that build up between people who genuinely love each
other.

This process has all of the benefits of wrestling in imagination, plus more. From those who have tried physical wrestling,
we have some reactions, some awarenesses: "I experienced how
strong I was." "I experienced how powerful my wife was." "I
found myself wishing my partner was not as strong as he was."
"I wished that I were stronger." "I was eager for my own physical strength to be put to the test." "I noticed the liability of my
overweight." "I loved waiting for just the right moment and
putting all my strength into a hold." "I noticed how tired I
grew." "I was astonished at my partner's cleverness and skill."
"I had to admit that I was at heart a dirty fighter." "I found that
I wanted to tell them not to trust me." On and on go the revela-
tory comments.

For some physical wrestling turned out to be spiritually special, too, in a symbolic way. One woman, after wrestling with
her fiancé, realized "to be that open, that vulnerable, that close
to another human being, to feel their sweat, their breath, and
accept it all—that requires special trust."

When married partners' love relationship is a conscious or
unconscious source of conflict, the wrestling may well move
into sexual experience. Wrestling, a primitive expression of as-
sertiveness, seems to touch something deep in people that appears to be connected to the age-old struggle between lover
and beloved and lets it be lived out in the world at this moment. During the wrestling, partners may discover places of
mistrust in each other.

The wrestling may allow them to break through their mistrust. The normal stages of a wrestling experience seem to include separateness and competition, then trust, cooperation, and union.

The format of the physical wrestling prayer follows the five steps previously outlined except you wrestle physically with a partner rather than in your imagination.

Afterwards, share your feelings and reactions and whatever you learned about yourself or your partner.

Chapter 19

Groaning, Screaming, and Weeping

A surgeon came into her patient's hospital room after an operation that had required a long incision in the intestinal area. "One very important thing to remember," she said to the man in the bed, "if you want your incision to heal, avoid sneezing, coughing, and laughing because these actions involve strong, violent muscular responses in the area of your incision."

Sometimes we forget how connected our body parts are to each other. We tend to associate sneezing, laughing, coughing, yawning, sighing, yelling, groaning, singing, and such with the mouth alone. Yet each of these actions involves much of our body. Notice, for example, how your whole body prepares itself for a sneeze. You can usually tell five or six seconds before you sneeze that your muscles and lungs and diaphragm are getting ready. Or next time you yawn notice how your stomach distends itself slowly but forcefully to facilitate the yawn.

This chapter focuses on the bodily activities of groaning, screaming, and weeping as settings for prayer, especially during time of extreme pressure or burnout.

Showing Compassion to Yourself

The psychological dynamics behind this form of praying begin with the realization that sometimes life is rough, pains are heavy, tasks are overwhelming, and therefore you have a right to feel sorry for yourself. Crying, screaming, and groaning are ways of showing compassion to yourself.

A counselor told the story of a college freshman who had all the symptoms of *anorexia nervosa*; she worried about getting fat plus her strong attraction to eating, so when she did eat she usually vomited her meal almost immediately afterward. Typical of adolescent girls, who seem to be the population segment most afflicted by this illness, she felt guilty about growing into adulthood and becoming a sexual being. This young woman, who was suffering from malnutrition and weighed less than eighty pounds, described to the counselor the miserable details of her life. She spoke unemotionally with an almost clinical detachment from herself. She told the counselor, almost proudly, that she never cried.

By this time the counselor himself was almost in tears, feeling a deep compassion for this young woman who was literally killing herself. Not knowing where to begin the therapeutic process, he simply asked the girl, "How would you feel if you had been sitting in my chair and heard what you just said about yourself?" The young woman said, "I'd feel very sorry for her," and then silently began to cry.

Sometimes it is a healthy thing to feel sorry for yourself, to feel compassion and weep for yourself. Feeling sorry for yourself sounds like a very natural response, and it often is. Unfortunately, many people were told by their churches and their parents to quit feeling sorry for themselves. Or, "if something hurts, offer it up to God." A healthier alternative is to offer your pain to God *and to groan or cry or scream as you offer it*. Thus as you make your spiritual and religious affirmation, you also give yourself some psychological and physical relief from the pain. Let the groaning be a sign of compassion for yourself.

Groaning, Sighing, and Moaning

A strong groan begins with a deep breath that distends and seems to fill the lower intestines. The pressure, felt there and then pushed out, meets momentary resistance at the throat, where the sound of the groan begins. When the throat is fully opened, the contained air rushes out and, as it passes the voice box, creates the sound we usually associate with groaning.

A groan is generally much stronger, louder, and more forceful than a sigh. A groan's objective is also different from that of a sigh. Usually a sigh symbolically acknowledges relief, "I'm glad that's over." One sighs with relief when, for example, the difficult exam is finished, the long assignment is turned in, the crucial interview is over, the critical medical report arrives and says "not malignant," the child remembers all the lines in the school play, you are not called upon to do something you feared, and so on. In each of these cases a sigh would be an appropriate sign that the body and mind feel relief and gratitude.

In contrast, the groan is most appropriate not when the pressure is taken off but *while it is still on.* The groan is like a valve that releases a strong overflow of pressure or pain while the pressure or pain is still building up. No matter how distasteful or disapproved the pressured feeling may be, let it come out of you. Otherwise, like garbage when kept inside indefinitely, it develops a repulsive odor that eventually fills every part of one's house.

Moaning, a gentler form of groaning, usually begins when the strong overflow of pressure or pain lessens. Although the pressure or pain is still present, it no longer has the burst of intensity that tends to produce a groan. Moaning signals a continuous but not quite intolerable level of pain or pressure. Moaning has a self-comforting quality and can generate the effects of a continuously voiced mantra. Moaning also helps to release anxiety.

The Groaning Prayer

The groaning prayer follows the now familiar five steps.

First, get in touch with the pressure, pain, frustration, anger, fear, or whatever strong feeling you want to release. Name it and own it as yours—as something inside you that needs to get out.

Second, ask God for the capacity to release whatever feeling may be overwhelming you at this time.

Third, begin groaning, and intend with your groaning to release the feelings that need to be released, so that as you exhale you groan these feelings out of you. You may find it helpful imaginatively to picture these feelings tied or attached to your groan. Groan until you feel some sense of relief.

Fourth, after you have groaned for a sufficient length of time—minimally five to ten minutes—thank God for the experience and for the continued compassion and care that God shows to you.

Fifth, reflect for a few moments on what the experience meant to you, how it might have affected you, and any insights about yourself you may have had.

Releasing Pressure

The groaning prayer may be used regularly, at set times, with great effectiveness. A supervisor in charge of a department builds up much frustration at work each day. He discovered that on days he spent part of his half-hour drive home doing the groaning prayer, he pulled into his garage much more relaxed than usual and did not need to take out his frustrations from work on his wife and children. So he decided to make the groaning prayer an essential part of his journey home every workday.

Groaning is a valuable pressure releaser for people who are in jobs and relationships that are not optional. For example, superiors, administrators, management personnel, nurses, teachers, and parents cannot avoid situations that generate pressure, conflict, and frustration daily, almost hourly. Groaning does not eradicate the source of the pressure—nothing can do that as long as the person remains in that type of job or relationship—but it can deal with the overflow of pressure as it builds up.

One caution about groaning: it is a rather noisy process and so it should be carried out where no one else can hear (for example, in an automobile with the windows closed). Or, if others must hear your groaning, give them advance warning that the groaning they will hear for the next ten minutes is not a call to them for help. This same caution also applies to the screaming prayer.

The Screaming Prayer

Screaming differs from groaning in this: screaming implies *there is something important you want to tell the world.* Screaming (or shouting or yelling) means making your voice heard in the world.

Some of the women in a group took one of their members to a deserted beach. She was a young, single woman who all through childhood had been told by her parents that she was selfish and that nobody would ever like her. At the beach she became very self-conscious, so the other women said they would go off for a while to let her be alone at the beach to scream. They told her to scream something important. At first she began speaking her message in a normal voice, but the more she allowed herself to believe her message was important, the louder her voice became. "I am not selfish," she shouted at the top of her lungs. Over and over she shouted these words out across the breaking waves, affirming what she wanted to say to the world to undo the hundreds of times her parents had spoken the opposite message.

A funny incident happened while she was shouting. Some fishermen in a boat offshore misunderstood her words, "not selfish," to be "got shellfish?" and they shouted back, "No shellfish today!" The unintended exchange with the fishermen made her laugh, and when her friends returned, they found her smiling.

It cannot be stressed enough that groaning and screaming prayers are meant to deal with feelings that might seem socially totally unacceptable. Even though other people may be unwilling to accept your fury, your disgust, your terror, your vulgarity, your lust, or your pettiness, God accepts you unconditionally as you are in every moment of your life. There is no need to hide anything from God. Scream your anger, or whatever is trying to possess you, at the skies. Scream for your health. Scream for your cleansing. Scream for the energy that cannot now flow within you. Express your feelings. Hold on to the healthy ones; let go of the destructive ones. Getting rid of such strong feelings is essential to the healing process, especially for those overwhelmed by pressures or suffering from burnout. God wants your health and wholeness.

Although the screaming prayer is recommended here for people near burnout, it may be used by anyone as a strongly affirmative prayer. One husband whose job required he spend a lot of time away from home would often roll down his car window as he drove along a deserted highway and shout his wife's name for all the world to hear, "I love you, Sandy Whitehouse." He found the practice very satisfying. Making one's voice—one's needs, beliefs, and wishes—heard in the world takes courage and takes practice.

Singing

Loud singing is another way of screaming or shouting. Singing is socially more acceptable and is especially satisfying in a shower, a gym, or the mountains, where the acoustics add a marvelous reverberation to the human voice.

A scholarly man said he didn't dare sing loudly in church,

though he wished he had the courage to do so. But when he went out on the mountainside alone, he felt free to sing. There he didn't hide his voice the way he did in church. On the mountainside he got in touch with his right to sing in the world. Sometimes he played with the power of his voice. Sometimes he sang songs he remembered; at other times he simply made up his own words and music. It proved to be a very spiritual time for him there.

The Crying Prayer

While groaning may express an overflow of feeling and screaming is meant for shouting something important to the world, crying (weeping, wailing) usually reflects the depth of one's anguish, sorrow, or compassion.

For all those suffering from burnout, crying is very important. Crying is to be encouraged. Let yourself cry loudly, noisily, and physically. Let your body become involved; roll around; beat on something with your fists. It announces your anguish and compassion to the world—and to yourself. If you cannot cry for your own woundedness, then cry for the wounds of others.

Tears are the sign of someone hurting. Tears can also wash away some of the hurt. Tears, crying, and moaning are healing forces. They help lay the hurting to rest and allow more hopeful images to surface.

Since it is not possible to "program" tears and weeping, it is difficult to plan a crying prayer in advance. Sometimes when you feel the nearness of tears, you can put aside some time and space to let your feelings surface and let the hurting experience happen as fully as possible.

Often the crying prayer happens spontaneously, unpredictably. After it occurs, you can thank God for the experience and take a moment to reflect on how it may have helped heal you.

Chapter 20

Squeezing and Hugging

In a workshop on stress a movement therapist suggested squeezing a tennis ball or a smaller rubber ball in times of heaviest psychological pressure. The purpose of squeezing was to relieve tensions and to help keep muscles relaxed.

In doctors' and dentists' offices people spontaneously squeeze the arms of the chair when they anticipate moments of pain. People feel an impulse to squeeze the driver's wheel when moving through heavy traffic. People squeeze things or wring their hands when they are upset or in grief. People squeeze another person's hand in times of fright. One little girl said she squeezed her fists together to help tolerate the pain of being scolded by her mother and her teacher. Children also squeeze their hands in prayer when they are "praying hard."

The Squeezing Prayer

To carry out the squeezing prayer, find a squeezable ball, one that will withstand a lot of presssure. (Handballs are almost universally effective.) To build consciousness that the ball will be part of your prayer, you may want to wash it ceremonially, mark it with special words or symbols, keep it in a special place, or carry it with you.

To do the prayer during times of pressure, keep the ball in

your hand. As you squeeze it, be conscious of the stress that is coming into you, of wanting to release this stress through the squeezing, and of directing a prayer toward God for your health. Let your prayer to God be for energy and wholeness as well as for release from the pressure of the moment.

How and When to Use This Prayer

The value of squeezing is that it may usually be carried on in the midst of stressful activity. Thus stress is released (by squeezing the ball) as soon as it is being generated, so it never gets a chance to build up to overwhelming proportions.

A woman whose job it was to telephone people to remind them their bills were unpaid was often subject to strong feelings through the frustrations or verbal abuse she received from the people she called. So as she sat at her telephone, she squeezed a handball, consciously allowing the feelings coming into her to pass right out of her system through the ball.

You may squeeze a ball in a variety of ways, such as with one hand, with both hands, between your knees, or under your heel (while sitting).

Hugging

Hugging is a form of squeezing. We naturally hug someone who is frightened or hurting. Some teachers report that hugging a child who has gone out of control is very effective. One teacher explained that when you hug young children who have gone out of control, they do not get frightened as one might expect. Rather, after a few moments of struggle and resistance—probably testing the teacher's strength and acceptance of them—they relax in the hugging and grow calm.

For those in burnout being squeezed or hugged somehow symbolically indicates someone wants to keep them from being shattered or fragmented. One woman was walking on the beach with a friend who had been going through a very stress-

ful period in her life—divorce, change of jobs, and moving to a
new home. There in the privacy and power of the ocean she began to cry uncontrollably. Spontaneously, the woman hugged
her friend. "The way she clung to me," the woman explained,
"I could tell she wanted me to hold her. I felt I was helping
hold her in one piece until she could pull herself together."
The holding somehow kept the friend's anxiety from tearing
her apart psychologically and from leaving her totally fragmented and wiped out. The woman's physical expression of
caring also allowed her friend enough time to recenter herself
and face her stressful situation. Here energies were shared in
order to reunify what had been fragmented.

When you need a hug and have no one to hold you, you
might try hugging yourself. "When I was a little girl and got
frightened," a young woman explained, "my big sister would
hug me. Now that I live alone, I often don't have someone to
hug me, so I hug myself. I hold myself together tightly, remembering how I was held as a child. In this way I comfort
myself."

The Hugging Prayer

To do hugging prayerfully during times of burnout, you may
follow these three steps. First, as you hug be conscious of the
stress and fragmentation that is threatening you or the person
you hug. Second, be conscious of wanting to hold yourself or
the person to keep you or them from totally fragmenting.
Third, connect yourself to God with a prayer for wholeness and
health.

Part V

Prayerways: Interpersonal Presence

Chapter 21

Affirming Others

Dr. Gerald Jampolsky, a psychiatrist who works with children who are terminally ill or who have suffered catastrophic illness, tells his patients that one of the best ways to heal yourself is always to be in a situation where you can help another person. He tells of one hospitalized eight-year-old boy who was paralyzed after having been run over by a tractor. The boy could not even speak, though he could use his left arm. A very young child in the same ward had been crying incessantly and nothing seemed to be able to stop him. In a moment of inspiration the eight-year-old's mother picked up the crying baby and brought it over to her son, who cradled him in his left arm. The crying ceased. The eight-year-old later told Dr. Jampolsky he remembered his advice and he was happy that even though he was paralyzed he could help someone.

Jane, a seventeen-year-old, had also learned the secret healing power of helping others. Whenever she felt lonely or had a lost sense of her own value, she helped others in a unique way. She affirmed the qualities she saw in others, and when she told others about their good qualities, she began to experience her love for them in a more alive way. Often after she had named a quality in someone else, she realized she possessed some of that quality, too.

Sometimes, Jane found, others are very aware of fears and inadequacies. Being in touch with her own fears enabled her to help them. When she described how her own fears and inadequacies felt to her, the other person who felt the same way also began to feel less lonely, less disconnected to people.

Affirming Others as a Prayer

Affirming others is a very special kind of prayer. It says to God, "I may not feel very good about myself or my situation right now, but at least I can affirm the gifts I perceive in other people." There are two stages to this prayer form: a silent, inner recognition of an affirmation about another person and a spoken affirmation made in the presence of that other person.

The silent prayer may be done reflectively by considering the persons with whom you frequently interact. These may include anyone from a bus driver or a supermarket cashier to your spouse, children, parents, or close friends. First, choose some person to reflect upon and do so, noting the qualities in them you would like to affirm. Second, visualizing them present to you, speak your words of affirmation. Third, ask God to bless them and to keep them whole and holy. You may also ask a blessing for yourself from God.

The spoken stage of this prayer involves actually saying your affirmation in person and following it with some expression of gratitude—to the person and to God.

The Power of Affirmation

Affirming others is a powerful way of building up the total body: all of us joined, sharing in the life of the universe and participating in the life of God.

The power of affirmation is seen by comparing the effects on students of teachers who teach by affirmation and teachers who teach by criticism. The critical teacher pointing out only failures often runs the risk of demoralizing students; the teacher who conscientiously reflects a student's positive qualities nurtures motivation and encourages students to reach further than they normally might.

Even weaknesses, fears, and failures can be viewed in a positive light, as part of human nature and as part of an individual's process. Something you experience "in process" means you won't always be stuck with it as you are now. You will work through the problem; you will overcome the weakness; you will develop the necessary skills.

Affirmation of others might sometimes be mistaken for flattery. However, telling people the potential you see beginning to bloom in them is very health giving. Many people will not have realized the truth of what you say until you recognize their potential and speak of it to them.

People remember what you say to them about themselves; they have a sense whether or not what you say is true or could become true. Hearing you affirm them, they learn to affirm themselves. They also learn to affirm you in return. And in this exchange the love bond between people is strengthened.

We all need somebody to believe in us. And we like to hear that belief expressed. No one needs someone to believe in them more than those experiencing burnout. Hearing someone they value express a hope for them can act almost like a self-fulfilling prophecy to discouraged people.

A psychologist told an elderly woman patient that she was strong. "If your relationship were to end," he said, "it would be painful, but you wouldn't be devastated by it." When the separation actually happened and the patient doubted her own ability, she remembered her therapist's affirmation of her. "I realized there was someone who believed in me," she said, "and it helped me believe in myself."

Affirmation of Others as Self-Healing

Being able to affirm another—to believe in another person—is also self-healing. In affirming others you also learn ways to affirm yourself. In speaking aloud affirmations of others you begin to listen to your own words and may discover they contain levels of meaning and information for you. In affirming others you are affirming at least your own care for others, your own wisdom, and your ability to observe qualities in others, all of which are deserving of affirmation in you.

Affirming others and affirming yourself eventually blend into a well-balanced care for self. As psychiatrist M. Scott Peck wrote in his book, *The Road Less Traveled*:

> It is actually impossible to forsake our own spiritual development in favor of someone else's. We cannot forsake self-discipline and at the same time be disciplined in our care for another. We cannot be a source of strength unless we nurture our own strength . . . not only do self-love and love of others go hand-in-hand but ultimately they are indistinguishable.*

* (New York: Simon & Schuster), p. 83.

Chapter 22

Person Next to Me

A variation on affirming others, a prayerful activity that can be done silently, involves sending loving messages from your heart to the people you meet. Social workers and other people in the helping professions, such as teachers, counselors, and often parents, at times feel overwhelmed by the fear that all the caring they show to others really doesn't make any noticeable difference in the world. "Week after week I let myself be eaten away," explained one social worker, "but all my loving and caring seems to have no impact. It's like beating my head against a brick wall."

It is typical of persons in burnout no longer to notice the little changes and transformations that actually do happen among the people they serve and only to be in touch with the tedious experience of their own daily routine.

The Value of Anonymity

The prayer being suggested here allows the burned-out person to direct his or her caring and loving—since caring and helping seem to be of the essence to persons in the helping professions—more anonymously.

Loving an anonymous person seems somehow easy and nonthreatening. It also allows the burned-out person to get back in touch with caring. One woman near burnout described her experience:

> I was riding home from work on a bus, feeling exhausted and sorry for myself, when I became fascinated with a little old woman sitting across from me. I got to wondering who she was and if she was tired, too. I found myself in my mind asking caring questions about her, studying the lines of her face and her movements. I began letting my feelings for her flow out of me and I felt my heart opening in a way I hadn't felt in a long time. She was nobody I knew, nobody in particular, but loving her in silence did wonders for my spirit that day.

Expressing your loving energy even in silence and even to strangers allows you to come alive and to make spiritual connection with them. Perhaps it is the very anonymity of the other person—they make no demands and have no expectations of you—that allows your caring to flow so freely.

Stopping in Kindness

A young woman who had finished her grocery shopping and was hurrying out of the supermarket with arms full of grocery bags noticed an older woman who had slipped and fallen coming in the door. Although she didn't want to get involved, she could tell the woman was scared, so she put down her bags and went over to her. It seemed she had twisted her ankle. When a clerk came over, the young woman told him to get a chair from the office so the older woman could sit down. She also told him to get the manager. Once the old woman realized she would be cared for, the younger woman left, feeling very good inside and taking these good feelings away with her. "I liked the me I had been," she said.

The woman enjoyed the experience of caring for someone she did not know. It put her in touch with how much she liked caring for people and she realized how important it was for her to have an outlet for the caring, helping part of her. She said, "The whole experience was a gift to me," surprised at how quickly it all happened and at how strongly she was aware of herself as a caring, comforting person. Being in touch with a part of her she liked, she could affirm herself in that experience. It made her realize she could always make time in her life for caring and comforting. "In putting aside my own weariness for a few moments," she said, "I forgot I was tired."

Even though this woman acted out her feelings of care and love, it is not necessary always to do so in order to perform the love the person next to you prayer. It is enough to focus your thoughts on the person, allow yourself to feel caring toward them, and ask God to bless them.

In the Mirror

It is also possible to do this prayer looking in the mirror at yourself. Pretend you are looking at yourself as if you were the person next to you. How would you describe yourself? What are your caring reactions to yourself? What are some of the positive qualities or potentials you see in the face in the mirror? Let yourself affirm them and thank God for them.

Chapter 23

Contacting a Friend

"If you're feeling sad and lonely . . . call me," begin the lyrics of a popular song of the sixties, offering wise advice to those under pressure or burnout. One of the most effective ways to relieve emotional pressure and to reopen channels of psycho-spiritual energy is through interpersonal contact with a friend or loved one.

One man from Rochester takes out his book of telephone numbers when he feels more than usually discouraged or pressured by his work. "I treat myself to three long-distance phone calls to friends I haven't seen in years," he said. "I usually tell the person I call that I am discouraged or exhausted and that I need some cheering up. They never fail me. By the time the third call is over, I feel a new sense of life and hope. I thank God for friends like them."

He explained that he also sometimes phones the same friends when he is especially happy or after an important success. "That way they know I have a positive and energized side, too, that I'm not always discouraged or down."

One single woman, when pressures get too much, goes for a weekend visit to a friend who lives at the ocean. "Those weekends are better than a vacation because at the ocean I have a friend who cares about me and is willing to let me pour out all my worries."

Making personal contact with another human being who is significant to you—by letter, phone, or visit—is a healing action that we have all experienced. Fortunate is the person who has a friend ready to stand by, firmly loving in time of trouble. For the burned-out person having someone who cares is crucially important while treading the arduous pathway back to wholeness. Making contact with such a person may easily be transformed into a prayerful activity.

Contacting a Friend Prayer

As you begin the phone call or visit, offer the experience to God as a prayer for energy. Affirm to God that in making the contact you are opening yourself up to be filled, through this person, with a gift of energy. Express your wish to be whole and healthy and your need for human contact in the process.

Next, simply enjoy the reconnecting with your friend. You may even wish to say this meeting is like a prayer time for you, that you want it to be a time for releasing your pressures and burdens, and for restoring hope, enthusiasm, and energy in your spirit. Psychologically, saying something like this helps clarify, for you and your friend, the healthy potential this contact can have for you and gives your friend a clear message about what is expected from him or her.

Afterwards, when you hang up the phone or when you are on your way home, thank God for the gifts that came to you while you were with your friend.

Being the Helper

It can be just as prayerful an activity to visit or phone someone who is discouraged or burned out with the intention of consoling and supporting them, even if you are in a similar worn-out state yourself. In either case you are affirming the spiritual power of human presence and communion.

Older people are especially appreciative of visits from younger people. One very pressured young man weekly drops in for coffee and chat with an elderly woman in the neighborhood who lives alone. Many times near the end of a visit she will tell him that he is like a miracle in her life. He, in turn, by releasing psychospiritual energy in her, discovers he too feels more alive. And so goes the marvelous facilitating of energy that happens when people connect their spirits in the service of wholeness and love.

Chapter 24

Touching

Burnout can happen in marriages and families as well as in other situations. Frustration with a partner, a parent, or a child can sometimes build up over months and years to a point of emotional and spiritual exhaustion. It is a drain on a family member's energy constantly to deal with, for example, young persons who refuse to keep their rooms clean and orderly, a mother who constantly nags and is never satisfied, a husband who refuses to acknowledge his feelings but keeps everything to himself, or a wife who puts herself down day after day and effectively cancels out everyone else's joy in life. Situations like these, when never confronted, often provide such an energy drain that the spouses sometimes feel divorce is the only answer, or young people feel the only way to release the pressure is to run away, to escape. The pain of such daily emotional wounding—reopening again and again these same wounds—becomes intolerable, since people seem not to be able to stop poking at these sensitive wounds in themselves and others. Emotional poking generates only more pain.

Touching invites healing of such wounds. Have you ever looked at a sleeping child and thought about how a few hours ago you were so frustrated you were ready to scream at the child because you had to call a dozen times before getting a response? Now asleep, the child looks peaceful and trusting, and you are touched by feelings of love. So you touch the child; you touch the miracle.

The Touching Prayer

Everything we touch is a miracle, if we could only see things the way God sees them. Let yourself enter into an awareness of what it is you touch. Then thank the Lord for the gift of this miracle. Say it in one simple word, "Thanks." That's all you need to do to begin to release spiritual energies within yourself.

These, then, are the three simple steps to the touching prayer, wherever and whenever you use it:

1. Lovingly touch something.
2. Become aware, as much as you can, of the miracle it is.
3. Thank God for it.

You may use any part of your body for touching. Hands can lovingly touch, of course. Feet can touch, too, as well as shoulders, backs, and hips. But so can noses (as the Eskimos know) and lips (as we all know). The make-up kiss after a conflict is an example of the first step of a touching prayer. So is the touching or kissing of a sleeping child. To this first step of touching in a loving context add a moment of awareness of what you are touching, and then thank God for the experience.

How do you do the third step? What do you say thanks for? Any number of things. For example, give gratitude for your renewal of wonder at what you are touching, for the joys and sorrows you have shared with what you are touching, for an awareness of how you may have squandered this gift before now by not seeing it, not appreciating it, wasting it, and so on. Say thanks for the ways you can express love through touching, for the fact that you are learning to touch more consciously, and for the forgiveness and reconciliation that touching implies.

Enriching Awareness

If you notice that touching a particular person, say, a spouse, is significant in reversing the tides of your burnout and opening you to a renewed flow of energy, then you may want to enrich the awareness step. To do this, it helps to relive, for example, the very first time you touched. Recall the occasion and its details as well as your emotions at the time. You may also relive other touching "firsts," such as the first hug, the first time you kissed or were kissed by the other, or the first lovemaking experience. You may also recall other moments of touching during painful and stressful times that were healing, helping, and comforting. You may also recreate in your imagination moments of joyful touching that happened during times of play, work, eating, or dancing. All of these touching moments involved your being together, your physical connectedness, as well as your spiritual union. Look again at the many ways you have shown love to the other and been energized by physical touching.

People suffering from burnout may not yet be able to maintain such a meditative focus, perhaps because they are still too depressed, anxious, exhausted, or frightened. In this case they can follow a more direct form of the touching prayer by going as deeply as they can into the details of the object they touch.

Things to Touch

While the most powerful touch objects generally seem to be humans, other touch objects can prove very effective. Pets are universally regarded as creatures with whom people may freely exchange the communication of touching. Other common touch objects include trees, rocks, plants, buildings, furniture, rugs, and anything else that offers a variety of textures. Each touch object offers a kind of connectedness with energy sources, a grounding with the earth, and perhaps a personal memory.

At a workshop a group of women, most of them near the brink of burnout, were each handed a stone and asked to handle it in order to become familiar with it, noticing details of texture, color, shape, and temperature. They were asked to study its details as if it were their very own special stone, something they could recognize anywhere, even if it were one in a pile of similar stones. After a minute they were asked to let their stone become a metaphor for themselves, to see how their own character and problems might be reflected in the stone. Finally, each one was asked to tell her life story up to the present as she saw it reflected in the stone.

Most of the women were energized by the experience. While they tended at first to see themselves reflected in their stone only as hard, cold, with jagged edges, resistant, alone, impenetrable, dull and gray, they began slowly to notice flecks of color imbedded in deeper levels of the stone, the gracefulness of its lines, its solidity, its strength, and the variety of textures that felt good to touch. After admitting to each other how they found themselves hard, resistant, and the like, they began to discover deeper, more positive, and attractive levels of themselves. When the session was over, no one left her stone behind. In fact, for some the stone became a special object in their life. One woman said, "I want to keep my stone in a prominent place in my room where it is clearly in view." She wanted to touch it and hold it often and remember the revelations it had helped disclose about who she was and who she could be.

Going Deeply

When touching natural objects prayerfully, the secret of effectiveness is to go deeply into them, exploring them in great detail as the women did their stones.

For example, while you are touching a tree, you can enrich your experience by noticing the sound of its rustling leaves, by feeling the different textures as you rub your hand and cheek against the bark, by smelling the earth around its roots, by seeing the shadings of color and the intricate veins in each leaf. Let yourself realize how miraculously complete one simple object can be. No architect could describe the myriad angles of the tree's branches; no artist could duplicate its colors.

Since each tree is also a home for other forms of life, each tree may be appreciated as the gift it is to the birds and insects, to the earth and the atmosphere, and to you and other humans.

Being Touched

Touching is one of the most primal sensory activities there is, and perhaps that is why it is such a healing experience. Almost all nursing and mothering care involves touch; and everyone, whether nurse or therapist, family member or friend, can look back on times when touch was extremely meaningful in a personal way. The comforting, healing, communicative effects of touch are such common occurrences that most people become all but indifferent to them.

By bringing being touched experiences into awareness, you may transform them into touching prayers. Simply follow the three steps listed previously: touching, awareness, and gratitude. The only difference here is that instead of being the one touching, you become the one touched.

Caring for Yourself

Another variant on touching prayerfully involves touching yourself. In this version you become both the toucher *and* the touched. Hands, face, and feet are the most obvious recipients of this prayer experience, though other parts of the body are not to be forgotten.

For example, take your right foot in your hand, look at it caringly, rub it, feel the muscles and bones beneath the skin. Take each toe and with a strong, firm motion pull it to its length. With the heel of your hand rub the sole of your foot or massage the bottom and sides of your foot with the pressure of your thumbs. As you rub your foot, let yourself become aware of how your feet cooperate with everything you do in your daily life—standing, walking, running, climbing, and dancing, connecting you with the earth and taking you wherever you want to go. Moreover, each foot cooperates despite aches, pains, tiredness, or being cramped in shoes all day long. Allow yourself to value the gift your feet are to you and the energy they dispense on your behalf. Afterward you may also want to treat your feet to a bath in warm water followed by a lotion rub.

According to acupressure theory and foot reflexology, all parts of a human body are directly connected to areas of the toes and feet, so massaging each part of the feet also helps relax the rest of the body.

Use the touching prayer as a way of doing loving things for your body. Express your care, for example, as you shower your body, shampoo your hair, or care for your fingernails. In each case transform the experience into a touching prayer by the three steps: touch, awareness, and gratitude.

As often as you use the touching prayer, it provides a relaxing, quieting, and loving prayer experience. It often evokes feelings of awe and wonder. It almost always produces a burst of energy and self-affirmation. It renews your contact with nature and with your own body—as channels of energy.

Chapter 25

Kything

A specially helpful form of spiritual connecting to others during times of burnout is called kything. The word, adapted by Madeline L'Engle, describes a center-to-center way of relating. To kythe (rhymes with scythe) with someone is to make your true self—sometimes called your spirit, heart, core, soul, or center—present to the other. It means your soul comes to someone, spiritually, without any disguises.

St. Paul was talking about this kind of presence when he wrote to the Ephesians, "When you believe in him, Christ comes to dwell in your heart" (Eph. 3:17). For Paul the arrival of Christ would be such a deep coming that it would feel like a being at home together; the believer and Christ would abide center-to-center in each other with completely open familiarity.

Center-to-center presence is also possible between human beings, and for this reason kything becomes a valuable aid for people in burnout or under severe pressure. This chapter suggests ways for people in burnout to understand and use the kything process. For some who have long been kything but didn't have a name for it, this chapter may help clarify the process and suggest other ways of utilizing the energies it can release, especially during stressful times.

A Special Kind of Centering

One way to understand kything is to see it as a special kind of centering. Centering, as we mentioned in Chapter 3, involves being present to one's deepest self and feeling at home in one's self. When people are in kythe, however, they are present to *another's* inmost self and at home in another's self. Thus to be in kythe with someone is to be centered in that other person or to have that other person centered in you and to feel at home in either case. Kything tends to produce a spiritual oneness, since it connects people soul to soul or heart to heart, thereby making possible a new kind of presence between people.

Physically, we are present to someone when we can reach out and touch them with our hands. Psychologically, we are present to someone when we are listening attentively to them or in communication with them. Spiritual presence refers to a connection that occurs on the level of the heart or spirit; it is usually called communion. Kything is an activity that brings about this communion. It involves focusing your spiritual presence *in* another person or their presence *in* you.

When Jesus says, "I live in the Father and the Father lives in me" or "I and the Father are one," he is describing what we call kything or being in kythe.

Sharing Energy

When we kythe with another person, because we are connected to their spiritual self with all its energy centers, we have access to their various energies. Kything enables us, especially when we are burning out, to tap incredible energy resources that are all around us. How many times have you looked at someone and said, "I wish I had her courage" or "I wish I had his patience"?

People who love you and care about you would happily

share their energies with you, especially those energies you lack right now. One friend may be strong in creativity and enthusiasm; another may have a strong sense of self; a third may be filled with forgiveness and compassion; still another may possess peace and strength; another may be strong in willpower and decisiveness. Kything offers a way for people to tap into each other's energies and share the spiritual wealth. Kything is a special way of loving that effects a sharing of energies.

You need not be physically present to someone in order to kythe with them, for your center or soul is not bound by the limitations of time or space. You can kythe with someone on the other side of town or on the other side of the world. You can kythe with your mother hundreds of miles away, your best friend in your neighborhood, or your child at school.

Kything is a natural spiritual process and anyone may learn to do it. It usually requires, first, that you know how to center, that is, how to get in touch with your center (spirit, heart, core, or soul), and, second, that you are willing consciously to move your center about.

The Kything Prayer

Although many people prefer to kythe during meditative periods, kything may be done prayerfully at any time, in any place. It need not interfere with your work, driving, study, play, or talking; in fact, kything may enhance them.

A young woman kythes every night before bed with some of her closest friends, people with whom she is no longer in physical contact but continues to be concerned about. A wife kythes with her husband whenever his job takes him on the road. On long drives the husband kythes with his wife, imagines her sitting next to him and talking with him. A student who tends to be disorganized kythes with a well-organized friend to share his calming and organizing qualities before a test or before speaking in public.

In each of these cases the kything may be done in a spirit of prayer. The kything prayer follows four natural steps. First, become centered. You may use any centering process you like for this as long as it puts you in touch with your inner self. Then ask God to fill you and your kything partner with the divine spirit.

Second, when you are ready, let your inner self find itself in the person with whom you wish to kythe. Use your imagination to help you make the transition. For example, you may picture yourself in his heart, standing beside her, or being held by him. Some people feel reluctant to place their spirit in someone else but feel comfortable inviting the other person's spirit to come into them. This is still kything. Either locus of union is acceptable.

Third, invite the energies you need to flow through your kything partner and into you. Let yourself be open to receive these energies, and as you welcome them remain restfully quiet if you are in meditation or go about your daily tasks if you are not in meditation. Notice any changes in your physical, psychological, and spiritual energies.

Fourth, thank God for the gift of life and energy that comes to you through the loving channels of others. Ask God to bless and energize those with whom you kythe.

At first kything may seem strange and difficult to some people, but with practice it becomes a natural and satisfying way of becoming present to others.

From another perspective, you may have been kything, or almost kything, for a long time. One Roman Catholic woman, when kything was explained, recalled how as a child each night she had invited her guardian angel to protect her, her patron saint to remain nearby, and Jesus, Mary, and Joseph to be with her and watch over her. For her these spiritual beings were present to her; they were right there in her room. Kything would take her childhood process one step further and invite these spiritual beings to come and live within her.

Choosing Someone to Kythe with

Choosing the right person to kythe with is important, especially in times of burnout. Kythe with those who are close to you, those to whom you feel you can fully entrust yourself. Children often choose to kythe with their parents. One child who was physically hurt and didn't want her friends to see her crying went off by herself and, in kythe, talked to her mother and heard her mother's comforting reply. Parents, too, instead of simply worrying about their children, can remain in kythe with them, sending them energies of strength, wisdom, kindness, prudence, and love.

One mother, concerned about her fledgling driver daughter, kythed grownup knowledge and driving know-how to her daughter on her first long solo drive. "Kything gave me a way of doing something more than being helplessly anxious about her," the mother explained. "Instead, I became actively involved in her task, not only by sending my energy and experience but by my spiritual presence." Because of her involvement, the mother was able to be calm and serene, knowing she had given her daughter "the best protection and energies I had."

Since burnout is characterized by anxiety, disorganization, and feeling overwhelmed and pressured, you can learn to kythe to people you experience as organized, peaceful, and serene and at the same time those who seem to possess the energy and efficiency you lack. In times of extreme need people spontaneously call upon God and the Saints hoping to find comfort and renewed energy. Kything, which takes such traditional prayer a step further, invites these spiritual beings to come into us and express their life in us.

Kythe with God, the Christ, special holy people, saints, and spiritual beings. Ask them to come into you bringing energies of life, vitality, and fulfillment. Voiced prayer to God and other beings implies and presumes a spiritual presence or connection between you and them. Kything simply makes the connection conscious.

In general, kythe with someone you love and trust and who would bring you the kinds of energy and serenity you lack. When considering kything, you might ask yourself two questions: What kinds of energies do I most need right now? Who among those I love and trust has plenty of the energy I need? These persons, then, are the ones with whom it would be valuable to kythe.

When you're feeling anxious, kythe with someone who would bring you serenity; when you're feeling disorganized, kythe with someone who would bring you stability and order; when you're feeling alone and unlikable, kythe with someone who would bring you companionship and a sense of worth. In a story mentioned in Chapter 21 a woman recently divorced who was moving to a new town and a new job found a friend who showed her caring and comfort. She learned also that she could carry this closeness a step further in kything with this friend, who she knew would comfort her in her anxiety and distress.

It is not necessary that the person with whom you kythe knows you are doing so. However, the kything experience seems to be intensified when both persons are aware of the activity and consent to the sharing of energy. Friends, family members, or couples who are to be separated for periods of time may agree to kythe with each other at certain specified moments of each day.

Kything with Nature

You may also kythe with animals and nature. Often the energies you lack may be found in a pet, a flower, or a tree. Connecting yourself with the earth's energies is a way of grounding yourself, of affirming the total bondedness of all creation. Here kything becomes a prayer of rooting; using it you connect yourself by means of your biological system to the roots of nature, thus breaking through the fundamental loneliness and apartness people often feel in time of burnout.

One young man during recuperation from burnout used to kythe with a large oak tree in a nearby park. Each day he would sit near the tree and put the center of his being in it. He became aware of how it lifted its branches toward heaven, opening its leaves to all the available energy of the sun, the air, and the rain while its roots, hidden from view, reached deep into the earth to tap the energies available to it there. The young man began to learn of his own need for deep connections to the earth—in caring for his body, which he had neglected—as well as an outward reach to sources of emotional nourishment available to him from his friends and family. The tree, he felt, gave him a sense of rootedness and also a desire to aspire toward holiness and wholeness.

Helping Others

You may also kythe with others in order to share your energies with them. Helping others allows you to become aware of your energy resources. It helps discouraged and self-disvaluing burned-out persons to realize they do have something to share. For example, when someone you know is very sick or dying, kythe yourself into them so they can feel your loving and your caring. Let the intensity of your prayer come out of your own frustration at wanting to share with the sick or dying person whatever health you do have and yet not being able physically to gift them with it. In times like these your spiritual presence may be all you can give them, and kything offers you a way of doing this, even when you cannot be physically present to them.

A young man, in addition to praying for the recovery of his uncle who had suffered a paralyzing stroke, used to kythe his uncle into himself as he jogged. Every morning as he jogged along the street, he would picture his uncle running healthily inside him, both of them using the same legs and body to run with. The young man, who wished to give his uncle the healing power of his spiritual presence, said that when he kythed with his uncle, the left side of his body—his uncle's paralyzed side—felt stiffer when he jogged. He didn't mind the stiffness, he said, because that reassured him that he really was in kythe with his uncle.

Kythe with people who are lost, confused, or frightened. Consciously put your spirit into their troubled space, then grow quiet and let flow into them your sense of caring, loving, and wanting to be connected to them. If they are physically present to you, you can ask them to be open to receiving what they need from you. Ask them to open their spirit and invite your spirit to flow into them. For example, ministers or priests may by the strength of their faith bring to grieving people peace and serenity through kything. Here it would be enough to ask the people in mourning to be open to sharing the peace and strength of the faith being offered.

Spiritual Communion

With practice, kything or spiritual presence will naturally become a strong motif in your spiritual life, whether or not you're in burnout. Kything also seems to transcend death. A lonely widow wished her dead husband were there to walk with her as she strolled around the family farm. Kything became a way for her to realize her wish. Now she speaks of walking around the farm with her husband in her heart. And a widower who intuitively discovered kything spoke to his deceased wife each night before he went to bed. He talked to her about his life and what was going on, and he invited her to participate in it through him.

The kind of spiritual communion made possible by kything seems central to the living in each other—the indwelling—that seems so important in Jesus' teachings and prayers. For example, in his prayer at the Last Supper, Jesus, referring to his followers, asked the Father "that they may be one as we are one.

With me in them and you in me, may they be so completely one that the world will realize that it was you who sent me and that I have loved them as much as you loved me" (John 17:22–23).

For Jesus, living in each other, in him, and in the Father was the summit of loving, the fulfillment of his single commandment "to love one another as I have loved you." Ultimately, to kythe lovingly is to participate in the divine life; it is to be at one with Jesus and the Father.

Chapter 26

Blessing

"God bless you" is a very common way of invoking divine favor upon someone. Prayers for those receiving baptism, confirmation, matrimony, and holy orders call for blessings and divine grace. Prayers on behalf of oneself also often take the form of asking a blessing from God or from saints or holy spirits. For example, after Jacob wrestled all night with the messenger of God, he would not let the angel go but demanded a blessing from him.

Familiar Blessings

God is not the only one who gives blessings. Humans bless each other every day but probably are not aware of it or never thought to call what they do a blessing. "Have a good day," "Good luck." "I hope everything goes well for you," "Bon voyage," and "Shalom" are all very common blessings humans exchange. The greeting cards people send each other on birthdays, anniversaries, holidays, or in times of grief are all blessings.

When you bless someone, such blessings, express a wish for their holiness, wholeness, healing, prosperity, success, and so forth. Thus traditionally in the Old and New Testaments children would ask a blessing of their parents; people would ask a blessing of their kings and priests; and students would ask blessing of their teachers. Jacob asked a blessing from his father, Isaac. Among these people such a blessing would effect a transfer of special spiritual power from the father to the son.

Jesus used a blessing gesture on children, on his disciples, and even on food. He blessed the loaves and fishes before the miracle of feeding the five thousand people, and he blessed the bread and wine at the Last Supper before he offered it to his followers as his own body and blood. People have always blessed their food.

What Is a Blessing?

Blessing usually involves a channeling of energy. It affirms that you wish to make an emotional and/or spiritual connection with another, that you wish energy to flow into them from you or into them from God through you. In this sense blessing someone is a very simple form of kything or spiritual presence.

Although blessing may be bestowed by written word, as in a letter or by word of mouth, blessings seem to generate more conscious awareness of the exchange of energy when some form of touching is involved. Some typical blessing rituals include placing your hands, palms open and facing down, on the head of the person to be blessed; cupping their cheeks; touching their shoulder (as in dubbing a knight); kissing them; touching with fingertips places on the body that need to be healed; and making the sign of the cross or some other sacred sign on their forehead, lips, throat, heart, hands, or feet.

The Blessing Prayer

You may ask another to bless you; you may offer a blessing to another; or you may exchange blessings with each other. While parents might naturally bless children, it is also possible to ask children to bless their parents or to bless each other.

In giving a blessing you may observe the following simple

steps. First, let the blessor and blessee both pause for a moment to get centered in themselves and to become conscious that they are to become channels of spiritual energy, affirming their connection with God.

Second, using whatever words and gestures seem appropriate, speak some words of blessing. Such words may be spontaneous or chosen from an already existing blessing formula, as in the prayers for administering the sacraments. Spontaneous blessings are encouraged. The blessing prayer may be as short or as long as you wish.

In this sense giving a blessing usually feels very natural. Parents seeing their children off to school might bless them by saying something like, "I hope you do well in your exam. God be with you." Or two people after an argument might bless each other by wishing for peace between them. If you don't know what blessing to ask upon a person, choose a blessing you would like for yourself.

Third, if there is to be an exchange of blessings, both may be done in immediate succession.

Fourth, the people involved can then remain quiet for a few moments, welcoming the blessing into them and thanking God for the opportunity to share energies. For example, a couple who have been apart for a time may greet each other initially with a kiss of greeting and good wishes, expressing their joy and love very simply. Then they may stand together in silence holding each other, conscious of the sacredness of the moment, of each other, and of their relationship. The mutual blessing may be done also when old friends or family members reunite, taking a moment after the exchanged words to relish the caring and blessing they feel toward each other.

An embellishment to this process is called the color blessing, where one person blesses another with one of the seven kinds of spiritual energy (see Chapter 2) and imagines a mantle of the energy covering, surrounding, or filling the person being blessed.

When to Use Blessings

Use blessings on special occasions or holidays among those with whom you share a spiritual closeness. When coming to visit or leaving, instead of merely shaking hands or exchanging a kiss, exchange a blessing; or let your kiss become a sign of blessing, that is, a flowing of spiritual energy between the two of you.

Someone gave the gift of a leather belt and on the inside of the belt wrote a blessing: "May you be surrounded by peace and love all the days of your life."

Putting children to bed is a naturally appropriate time and place for blessings. It affirms a spiritual bond in the family as well as the obvious physical bond.

Burned-out people can ask for blessings from their special friends and may be asked in return to give blessings to their friends. When you are burned out, it is helpful both to give and receive blessings. Giving a blessing lets you feel you still have something to give. Receiving one lets you feel supported, reassured, affirmed, connected, and therefore hopeful. Blessings speak to the present moment but also to time beyond this moment. To share a blessing with a friend—or even with a stranger—is to feel connected and nourished. It is a good experience for a soul who feels worn down to the bare bones.

Exchanging blessings helps remind us of the interconnectedness and interdependence of the entire human family. It is a sign that we are conscious of the spiritual needs we have and aware that such energies come to us often through other persons.

Summary

All the prayerful strategies presented in this book share a common purpose: to help you live a more fully functioning life on all three levels—body, mind, and spirit. We hope the book's message and content help to enrich your whole being and your whole experience of being and are an invitation to fullest life, even during times of severe pressure.

To stay alive during times of stress and burnout, we emphasized the need to care for all three human energy systems. When one or more of these systems becomes overstressed, it would be particularly helpful to nourish the remaining systems. While we are conscious most often of enduring physical and emotional stresses, we tend to forget the need to nourish the spiritual system, which could support the other two. For example, in the experience of grief or loss, psychological stresses of sadness, depression, and anger appear, as well as physical stresses, which sometimes result in headaches, tiredness, and lack of appetite. In situations like these a well-maintained spiritual system might make a significant difference in the success and ease of the emotional and physical healing process.

While the book takes a wholistic approach toward working through burnout, each of its sections focuses on a different piece of the whole—emotions, the reflective mind, the physical body, the spirit, and interpersonal experiences. Each of these pieces belongs to the totality, and the whole is more than the sum of its pieces. For it is to the whole person that divine grace is given. The call to holiness and the call to wholeness are ultimately simply different aspects of the same limitless and ever expanding call.

Within this call to holiness and wholeness, in each chapter we asked you to take what may seem like an ordinary moment or happening in your life and *with your intention* carry the experience into a communion that connects you with God and invites spiritual energy into you. In short, your intentionality makes the difference, transforming an otherwise ordinary moment into a prayer.

It is our hope that in these pages you have found new ways of making prayer a natural part of your daily life, new ways of experiencing your connectedness with God, new ways of tapping the deep resources of energy within you and around you, and new ways of seeing the inner connectedness between your energy and the energies of the universe. Or, as Henri Nouwen put it, "Prayer is not a pious decoration of life but the breath of human existence." *

* Henri Nouwen, *The Wounded Healer* (New York: Doubleday, 1972), p. 17.